MW01531105

END OF AN ERA

CHELSEA 2021/2022

CHRIS WRIGHT

End Of An Era
Chelsea 2021/2022
Copyright Chris Wright 2022
ISBN: 9798835464616
THE MORAL RIGHT OF THE AUTHOR HAS BEEN ASSERTED
Apart from any fair dealing for the purposes of research or private study, or criticism or review, as permitted under the Copyright, Designs and Patents Act 1988, this publication may only be reproduced, stored or transmitted, in any means, with the prior permission in writing of GATE 17, or in the case of reprographic reproduction in accordance with the terms of licenses issued by the Copyright Licensing Agency. Enquiries concerning reproduction outside those terms should be sent to the publishers. Email: enquiries@gate17books.co.uk

Typesetting and design: Mark Worrall
Cover artwork: Steph's Sketches
Rear cover photograph: Chris Wright
www.gate17books.co.uk

CONTENTS

ACKNOWLEDGEMENTS

The 5th Stand App (Chelsea FC), BBC Sport, Times Sport, Sky Sports, Sky News, Matt Law (Telegraph), James Robson (Standard Sport), Sami Mokbel (Daily Mail), Ben Jacobs (CBS Sports), Mark Worrall, Tim Rolls.

This book is dedicated to my wonderful wife Jo and my two beautiful children Jack and Emily.

INTRODUCTION

Following Chelsea was always inevitable growing up in the 1980's / 1990's. My dad started going to games in the mid 1960's and adopted the club when he moved to Fulham as a schoolboy. Even today he still speaks fondly about the famous team of Osgood, Hutchinson, Bonetti, Harris, Hudson etc and how magical it was at Old Trafford in the 1970 F.A Cup Final Replay and going on to win the European Cup Winners' Cup in Athens the following year.

My first game was February 10th 1990 at six years old. A league match against Manchester United and a 1-0 win thanks to Gareth Hall, a memorable day shared with my dad (Rick) and his two friends. A trip to the little club shop after the game, I was instantly hooked and quickly asked my dad when I'd next be able to go to a match.

During the early 90's I went to a number of games with my dad and two older brothers Steve and Dan and just loved the match day buzz. We'd often stand in 'The Shed' and take a foot stool with us so that I could see. We were often let in for free and told to crawl under the turnstiles by a steward. The smell of fried onions and burgers and hearing the crowd roar was fantastic and it often made me laugh when an announcement over the loudspeakers would inform a supporter that his wife had just gone into labour, always greeted with a big cheer!

PRE-SEASON

Despite Euro 2020 having already started, the Premier League fixtures for the 2021/22 season were released on June 16th. Games would always be changed later for television coverage but it's always a much talked about topic once they are released. Chelsea would face Crystal Palace on match day one at Stamford Bridge. On paper it looked a very tough first six games as we faced Arsenal, Liverpool and Tottenham away and Manchester City at home.

The first player to leave the club on a permanent basis was Fikayo Tomori. An academy graduate who had spent time on loan at AC Milan during the previous season. He decided that's where he'd like to stay and a deal was agreed. Fikayo posted on his Twitter account, 'Thank you for everything'.

Chelsea announced that the club would compete in a pre-season tournament with Arsenal and Tottenham. A MIND Series raising money to support better mental health. Chelsea would face Arsenal at the Emirates Stadium followed by Tottenham at Stamford Bridge. After impressing for Scotland against England at Euro 2020, midfielder Billy Gilmour joined newly promoted Norwich City on a season-long loan. We also said a permanent goodbye to Victor Moses after he joined Spartak Moscow.

Victor spent nine years at Chelsea and although he had various loan deals during his time he gained much respect when he returned to the club under the reign of Antonio Conte. He was instrumental as a right wing-back and vital to the team that won the Premier League in 2017 and F.A Cup in 2018.

Pre-season officially started back at Cobham on July 9th. It was mostly a mixture of academy players and returning loans. Most notably Tammy Abraham and Callum Hudson-Odoi were amongst the group. On the same day goalkeeper Willy Caballero announced via his Instagram account he would be leaving the club.

'It has been a pleasure and honour to defend this shirt'. Willy spent four years at Stamford Bridge.

All eyes were now firmly on the Euro 2020 final on July 14th. England were in the final of a major tournament for the first time since 1966. It didn't 'come home' in the end and Italy defeated England in a penalty shoot-out. Nevertheless it was a great tournament with some fantastic games. The use of VAR was refreshing and a huge improvement on how it was used in the Premier League. Italy were worthy winners with our very own Jorginho instrumental in midfield. Despite the disappointment I'm sure many Chelsea fans would agree that seeing club legend Gianluca Vialli so happy brought a smile to our faces. After everything he'd been through with his fight against cancer it was great to see him part of the Italian coaching team.

The day after, former blue Arjen Robben announced his retirement from football after a fantastic career. Although he was only at Chelsea a short while he was a joy to watch and that combination with Damien Duff is arguably the best we've ever had on the wings. Despite his injuries he was brilliant in our glittering success between 2005-2007 under Jose Mourinho. Lets not forget he also played his part in the 2012 Champions League Final!

Cult hero Olivier Giroud was the next to leave Chelsea on a permanent basis, heading to AC Milan for £2m including add ons. A true professional who had always been reliable when called upon.

'To all The Blues, to my team mates, to all my coaches, to the whole club, a huge thank you for these special moments. I'm starting a new journey with a light and happy heart. Our victories in the F.A Cup, Europa League and Champions League have been magnificent'.

I'm sure I speak for all Chelsea fans when I say thank you Olivier and thank you Arsenal!

17th July
Pre-season Friendly
Chelsea 6-1 Peterborough United
Cobham Training Ground

Chelsea Team: First-half: Cumming, Clarke-Salter, Chalobah, Sarr, Zappacosta, Barkley, Drinkwater, Alonso, Hudson-Odoi, Pulisic, Abraham

Chelsea Team: Second-half: Bergstrom (60 mins), Sterling, Miazga, Maatsen, Rahman, Gallagher, Baker, Ziyech, Loftus-Cheek, Broja, Ugbo
Chelsea Goals: Abraham, Pulisic, Broja, Ziyech (3)

Whilst COVID-19 vaccinations were taking place at Stamford Bridge and Mason Mount was away singing 'Sweet Caroline' with England team mates in Greece we had a game to play! A behind closed doors friendly against Peterborough United saw The Blues run out 6-1 winners. Tammy Abraham, Christian Pulisic, Armando Broja and a second-half hat trick from Hakim Ziyech got the goals. With many players still missing after the conclusion of Euro 2020 and the Copa America it was a team consisting of many academy and loan players.

The next day Chelsea announced the permanent sale of academy defender Marc Guehi to Crystal Palace for £18m. We would however be entitled to a sell on clause including the ability to match any bid accepted in the future by Crystal Palace. It came as a shock to many supporters especially after the sale of Tomori and an impressive loan at Championship side Swansea City the season before.

To everyone in the UK July 19th was known as 'Freedom Day' where all COVID-19 restrictions were now lifted. In football terms it meant all stadiums could now legally go back to full capacity. The squad flew out to Dublin for a pre-season training camp. We were due to play Droghead in a friendly match, it was cancelled at short notice due to COVID-19 concerns. The squad had a competitive game against each other which ended in a 1-1 draw. Armando

Broja and Callum Hudson-Odoi got the goals before the squad returned to Cobham. More first team players reported back, including Timo Werner, Kai Havertz, N'Golo Kante, Kurt Zouma and Mateo Kovacic.

27th July
Pre-season Friendly
Bournemouth 1-2 Chelsea
Vitality Stadium

Chelsea (4-3-4): Kepa (Mendy h-t), Sterling (Miazga h-t), Baker (Chalobah h-t), Sarr (Clarke-Salter h-t), Hudson-Odoi (Zappacosta 63), Drinkwater (Loftus-Cheek h-t), Gallagher, Alonso (c) (Rahman 63), Ziyech (Barkley h-t), Abraham (Ugbo 63), Pulisic (Broja h-t)
Chelsea Goals: Broja (71), Ugbo (76)

Bournemouth (4-2-3-1): Travers, Stacey (Camp h-t), Ibsen Rossi, Kelly (c) (Greenwood 82), Smith (Zemura 60), Marcondes (Glover 82), Kilkenny, Brooks (Saydee 71), Billing (Moriah-Welsh 82), Taylor (Edwards h-t), Solanke (Surridge 82)
Bournemouth Goal: Marcondes (66)

Leading up to the game, Chelsea sold another academy player, Lewis Bate, to Leeds United for an undisclosed fee. There was now a feeling this wasn't going to be the last academy player to move with first-team football and better pathways the key reasons.

1,200 Chelsea supporters made the trip to the South Coast on a Tuesday night to see The Blues in action for the first time since being crowned Champions Of Europe. They were certainly in full voice and for those watching on the 5th Stand App they could certainly be heard throughout. The game itself was played at a much higher tempo than many had anticipated and Conor Gallagher was the only Chelsea player to play the full 90 minutes. Marcos Alonso started the game as captain and Edouard Mendy finished it leading the team. Tammy Abraham had a couple of good chances in the first-half with Callum Hudson-Odoi and

Christian Pulisic also looking very lively.

We found ourselves 1-0 down midway through the second-half but responded very well with two quick goals. Armando Broja carried on his goal scoring run converting from close-range via a deflection after some good work from Baba Rahman. Ike Ugo netted the winner with a close-range header from a Ross Barkley corner.

The next day Chelsea announced the signing of goalkeeper Marcus Bettinelli on a two-year deal from Fulham. A back up goalkeeper was inevitable after Willy Caballero left the club.

The 2021/22 away kit was officially launched on July 29th. It came as no real surprise as many leaks were already on the internet. Chelsea were back in yellow and it seemed to generally be a hit amongst supporters.

AUGUST 2021

1st August
Pre-season Friendly – The MIND Series
Arsenal 1-2 Chelsea
Emirates Stadium

Chelsea (3-4-3): Mendy (Kepa 64), Zouma (Sterling h-t), Chalobah (Clarke-Salter 86), Rudiger (c) (Sarr h-t), Pulisic (Kante 64), Loftus-Cheek (Barkley 64), Kovacic (Drinkwater h-t), Hudson-Odoi (Rahman 64), Ziyech (Batshuayi 64), Havertz (Abraham h-t), Werner (Zappacosta h-t)
Chelsea Goals: Havertz (26), Abraham (72)

Arsenal (4-2-3-1): Leno, Chambers (Bellerin 71), Holding (White h-t), Mari (Kolasinac 71), Tierney (Tavares 71), Elneny (Lokonga 71), Partey (Xhaka 40), Pepe, Smith Rowe (Willock 71), Aubameyang (c), Lacazette (Nketiah 71)
Arsenal Goal: Xhaka (69)

The MIND Series kicked off with Chelsea facing Arsenal at the Emirates Stadium. With no away fans officially allowed to attend it was shown on the 5th Stand App with the cost going to the MIND Charity. On the day I was heading to Kings Cross station to pick up my nieces who had travelled down from Newcastle for part of the summer holidays. Me and my son Jack decided to pop to Arsenal and get a programme before the game started. I was surprised to see a number of blue shirts milling about and the number of ticket touts outside Arsenal underground station. There would be nothing new about Chelsea fans in the home ends against Arsenal which was often a common sight in the 80's and

90's.

Chelsea took the lead in the 26th minute as we hit Arsenal on the counter attack. Timo Werner was able to burst through, with only Pablo Mari back defending he was able to play in Kai Havertz who finished superbly into the top corner with his right foot.

There were chances for both teams with Emile Smith Rowe and Hakim Ziyech hitting the woodwork. Arsenal's biggest concern before half-time was Thomas Partey going off injured and trying to tame Callum Hudson-Odoi. With 23 minutes remaining Arsenal were back on level terms as Xhaka headed in Nicholas Pepe's corner. Chelsea regained the lead just minutes later as Tammy Abraham finished coolly after a defensive error from Hector Bellerin.

Arsenal felt they should have had an equaliser after Joe Willock's shot appeared to have crossed the line. With no goal line technology it wasn't given and Chelsea won the game 2-1. Next up was Spurs at Stamford Bridge.

Ticket details for the Super Cup Final against Villarreal were finally announced on August 2nd with Chelsea officially allocated just 2,000 tickets. Captain Cesar Azpilicueta was back at Cobham, joined by Mason Mount, Reece James, Ben Chilwell, Thiago Silva, Emerson and Jorginho. We also said goodbye to another academy graduate. Defender Tino Livramento joined Southampton in a permanent deal.

4th August
Pre-season Friendly – The MIND Series
Chelsea 2-2 Tottenham Hotspur
Stamford Bridge

Chelsea (3-4-3): Mendy, Chalobah (Miazga 80), Zouma (Ampadu 63), Rudiger (Sarr 63), Hudson-Odoi (Pulisic h-t), Kante (c) (Bakayoko h-t), Kovacic (Loftus-Cheek 63), Alonso (Zappacosta 63), Ziyech (Anjorin 63), Havertz (Abraham 63), Werner (Kenedy 63)
Chelsea Goals: Ziyech (16, 49)

Tottenham Hotspur (4-2-3-1): Gollini, Doherty (Aurier 80), Tanganga, Dier, Reguilon (Davies 73), Skipp, Hojbjerg (Winks h-t), Lucas Moura, Alli, Bergwijn (Scarlett 80), Son
Tottenham Hotspur Goals: Lucas Moura (56), Bergwijn (70)

The moment we'd all been waiting for, fans back properly at Stamford Bridge! With no official attendance released I'd guess there were around 25,000 – 27,000 and my first live game since 25th February 2020. Although it was only a friendly it was such a buzz to be back and you could feel it building up to kick-off. When the MIND Series was announced and COVID-19 restrictions were lifted it was an occasion I couldn't miss. My Dad unfortunately couldn't make it so a friend of mine was more than happy to take his ticket. Fans in attendance had to prove they'd had both COVID-19 vaccinations or provide a negative test result.

After finishing work I decided to get up there early to soak it all up and the queues outside the megastore were outrageous. I had a quick browse around and saw the new away kit in the flesh for the first time which I was very impressed with.

A quick hot dog down the Fulham Road before heading off to the Chelsea Pensioner Pub. It was 'so good, so good, so good' to be back in there. It was buzzing inside with fans singing songs as the DJ belted out the tunes. I went downstairs after finally getting a drink and caught up with Mark Worrall (Twitter @gate17Marco) and discussed the start of this book. Always good to catch up especially when it had been so long since I'd seen him. We decided to head to the ground around an hour before kick-off. Would never normally do this but there was a feeling it wouldn't be easy getting in the ground. As we got to the West Stand turnstiles to our amazement there wasn't any Covid-19 checks, we scanned our paper tickets and went straight in. Inevitably we went straight to the bar, soon the announcement was made the team would be bringing out the Champions League Trophy.

As we took to our seats it was most notable the Matthew Harding Lower tier was completely empty due to the rail seating work still not completed with those supporters relocated to the East Upper. It was great being back in my usual seat and seeing some familiar faces around us, you may not know all their names but you've celebrated some glorious moments with them over the years. Cesar Azpilicueta and the squad took to the centre circle and showed off the Champions League trophy with 'Champions Of Europe, we know what we are' quickly echoing around Stamford Bridge. A great moment, especially for those who couldn't get to Porto. Once the teams were out it didn't take long for the 'Where the fuck is Harry Kane?' chants responding to him allegedly not returning to Tottenham training in the week building up to the match.

Chelsea very much dominated the first-half with possession and chances. It came as no surprise that we took the lead on 16 minutes through Hakim Ziyech. It was a goal that all came from the ever impressive N'Golo Kante who captained the team on the night. He made a fantastic tackle in the middle of the pitch to intercept Lucas Moura, the ball broke for the Moroccan who hit a long-range shot into the bottom corner as the Tottenham defenders failed to challenge him. I don't think I've ever celebrated a goal in a friendly more! It was quite a carnival atmosphere with cheers at every pass a Chelsea player made. We were also up and down out of seats throughout the first-half as 'Stand up, if you hate Tottenham' rang round The Bridge.

Our second goal came shortly after half-time and it was Ziyech again. This time from close-range after some great build-up play from Werner, Havertz and Marcos Alonso. We deserved it but Thomas Tuchel was understandably making many changes involving players that were unlikely to feature come the start of the season. Lucas Moura and Steven Bergwijn got Tottenham back on level terms and although both teams had chances in the later stages neither team could find a winner.

With Fulham Broadway station closed it was a walk up to Earl's Court with streams of Chelsea fans heading in the same direction. It was great to be back and for me that was more important than any result. The talk on the train was all about Chelsea potentially signing a striker and the Super Cup Final.

11th August
UEFA Super Cup
Chelsea 1-1 Villarreal (Chelsea won 6-5 on penalties)
Windsor Park, Belfast

Chelsea (3-4-3): Mendy (Kepa 119), Chalobah, Zouma (Christensen 65), Rudiger, Hudson-Odoi (Azpilicueta 82), Kante (c) (Jorginho 65), Kovacic, Alonso, Ziyech (Pulisic 43), Werner (Mount 65), Havertz
Chelsea Goal: Ziyech (27)

Villarreal (3-4-3): Asenjo, Foyth, Albiol (c), P. Torres, Pino (Mandi 90), Trigueros (Gomez 70), Capoue (Gaspar 70), Pedraza (Estupinan 58), G. Moreno, Dia (Raba 85), A. Moreno (Morlanes 85)
Villarreal Goal: G. Moreno (72)

The lead up to the Super Cup Final was all about the imminent arrival of striker Romelu Lukaku after terms were agreed with Inter Milan. An exciting time and the race was on to see if he would be available to play in the first league match against Crystal Palace. Armando Broja had signed for Southampton on loan and there was still a lot of uncertainty regarding the future of Tammy Abraham. It was however all overshadowed in world football as Lionel Messi finally left Barcelona and joined PSG on a two-year deal.

As Villarreal beat Manchester United in the Europa League Final it would be them who Chelsea would face in the Super Cup Final. A trophy that had eluded us since 1998 when The Blues defeated the mighty Real Madrid in Monaco thanks to a late Gustavo Poyet winner. Since then defeats occurred in 2012, 2013 and 2019.

There was always going to be a huge interest in this game with easy access to Belfast for many. The official Chelsea allocation was just 2,000 tickets but many got them directly through UEFA and thousands more would travel without them. It was also the birth of a new song. To the tune of 'Heaven Is A

Place On Earth' by Belinda Carlisle

'Oh Roman do you know what that's worth,
Kai Havertz is the best on earth,
The silky German is just what we need,
He won Chelsea the Champions League'.

The big trophies are dished out at the end of the season but this was a great opportunity to go into the new season with even more confidence and put yet another cup in the ever growing Chelsea trophy cabinet.

The nerves were flowing before this one, although some describe it as a glorified Community Shield it was a trophy we hadn't won for 23 years. This was Chelsea's first ever competitive match against Spanish side Villarreal. The team selection included Trevoh Chalobah at centre back who Thomas Tuchel had been impressed with throughout pre-season and he most definitely deserved his opportunity. N'Golo Kante captained the team and Antonio Rudiger made his 150th Chelsea appearance.

Chelsea dominated the opening stages and it was the in-form Hakim Ziyech who opened the scoring on 27 minutes with a clever finish after Kai Havertz had done all the hard work on the left-hand side. Chelsea had other chances to increase the lead but there was an all-too-familiar sight with missed chances. As half-time beckoned Rudiger was harshly booked and as a result of a protest so was Thomas Tuchel on the touchline. Alberto Moreno had a great chance to equalise meeting a cross at the far post and hitting the cross bar. Hakim Ziyech who was having a very good game was replaced by Christian Pulisic due to a shoulder injury.

Havertz had a good opportunity at the start of the first-half but could only hit the side netting and Edouard Mendy was also called into action at the other end saving a Moreno shot onto the post. Chalobah was defending heroically but Villarreal looked more and more threatening. The equaliser came on 72 minutes and in all fairness it was a great finish from Gerard Moreno after a clever one-two. Chelsea could have cleared the ball better but the equaliser had certainly been coming.

Extra-time was inevitably nail-biting, I had a feeling it would go to a dreaded penalty shootout. The best chances fell to Chelsea, firstly Christian Pulisic frustratingly shot wide and then a ferocious shot from Mason Mount was palmed away. To everyone's surprise the last substitute in extra-time was goalkeeper Kepa Arrizabalaga replacing Edouard Mendy. It was obviously pre-planned as Mendy didn't look disappointed or surprised. Initially I was unsure as Mendy actually had a very good game.

Villarreal won the toss and the penalties would be taken in front of the their supporters with Chelsea taking the first one. Chelsea had lost their last two Super Cup Final's on penalties, would it be third time lucky for The Blues?

Havertz – saved, G. Moreno – scored, Azpilicueta – scored, Mandi – saved, Alonso – scored, Estupinian – scored, Mount – scored, Gomez – scored, Jorginho – scored, Raba – scored, Pulisic – scored, Foyth - scored, Rudiger – scored, Albiol – saved

Chelsea won 6-5 on penalties!

Another fantastic night in Chelsea history and an added boost going into the 2021/22 season. Chelsea are officially the first team in football history to win all four major European trophies twice. Not bad for a club that apparently has 'no history'.

14th August
Premier League
Chelsea 3-0 Crystal Palace
Stamford Bridge
Attendance: 38,965

Chelsea (3-4-3): Mendy, Chalobah, Christensen, Rudiger, Azpilicueta (c) (James 66), Jorginho, Kovacic, Alonso (Emerson 86), Pulisic (Havertz 82), Werner, Mount
Chelsea Goals: Alonso (27), Pulisic (40), Chalobah (58)

Crystal Palace (4-4-2): Guaita, Ward, Guehi, Kouyate, Mitchell, Schlupp (Anderson 57), Riedewald (Ray-Sakyi 76), McArthur (c), Zaha, Mateta (Benteke 57), Ayew

Despite the Super Cup success there was mixed feelings amongst supporters going into the opening game of the season. The club announced that the rail seating in the Matthew Harding Lower was still not completed and wouldn't be finished in time before the match against Crystal Palace. 908 supporters were told that a refund would be given and they'd get a complementary Champions League group stage ticket. Although much blame was put on the contractors this left a sour taste especially so soon after the Super League disaster of the previous season. If the club wanted to build bridges with supporters this was another huge setback with many fans looking forward to returning to Stamford Bridge for the first time in 18 months.

Right up until kick-off the club were contacting those affected as a ballot was taking place to relocate them to the new 'Westview'. Twitter was also certainly doing its thing! Fans tweeting and retweeting requests for spare tickets and it was great to see many got to the game.

The day after the Super Cup the official announcement was made that striker Romelu Lukaku was returning to Stamford Bridge on a five year deal for a fee of around £97m. It was a shame he couldn't make his second debut at Stamford Bridge but he had to quarantine before linking up with the rest of the squad.

The 'cfcuk' stall (opposite Fulham Broadway station) was back open for the first time since 8th March 2020. The fanzine had continued to be published throughout COVID-19 but on a personal note it was the first time my debut book 'Blue Days' was sold on a match day.

There was no display in the ground of huge banners and crowd-surfers out of respect. The club placed on the big screens the names of Chelsea supporters who had died over the previous 18 months which was a very moving moment.

Most notable absences from the team was the in-form Hakim Ziyech who came off in the Super Cup and N'Golo Kante although the issue wasn't reported as serious.

Kicking off the new season in the sun is how it should be, the weather was glorious. It was a very strong performance and with respect to Crystal Palace it was a stroll. Shortly before the half hour mark Mason Mount was fouled just outside the box, a free kick was given with Mason and Marcos Alonso standing over it. Marcos hit a sublime free kick up and over the wall beating the goalkeeper and ending up in the top corner. A fantastic moment and one to savour for all the fans inside Stamford Bridge.

With five minutes before half-time Chelsea doubled the lead. Christian Pulisic on hand after a neat one-two between Mount and Azpilicueta and goalkeeper Guaita could only parry the ball into the path of Pulisic who finished. The second-half continued to be one way traffic and on 58 minutes came the moment of the match. After playing in the Super Cup Final and making his Premier League debut it was 'written in the stars' for Trevoh Chalobah. Picking the ball up in his own half, driving forward he was urged to shoot from the Stamford Bridge crowd. A 30-yard shot into the bottom left-hand corner which went in off the far post was just an incredible moment. The crowd went wild as Chalobah had his head in his hands in disbelief as he was mobbed by the rest of the team. A clearly very emotional moment which he most certainly deserved as he was brilliant throughout the game and received the Man Of The Match award.

Palace finally had a shot on target but it was a very dominant Chelsea display where we could have scored more. Chelsea fans proceeded to sing in the direction of the Crystal Palace supporters; 'You're going down with the Arsenal'!

This was Trevoh Chalobah's response after the game; "I'm lost for words at the moment. I dropped to my knees and I was crying, really. It's amazing for myself and my family. I had to wait (for my chance at Chelsea) but for me it's important to work hard, stay patient and keep working to focus on your game and where you need to improve. This isn't enough, I need to do more and more and that's what I'm aiming to do".

The next day Chelsea played National League side Weymouth in a behind closed doors friendly at Cobham to give our large squad more match fitness going into a very busy season. Kepa, Thiago Silva, Zouma, Ampadu, Chilwell, James, Zappacosta, Emerson, Barkley, Batshuyai and Hudson-Odoi all featured in the game with Chelsea winning 13-0! Batshuyai (5),

Barkley (3), Hudson-Odoi (2), Thiago Silva and James were the first team players among the goals. No official line-up was released.

More media duties for new signing Romelu Lukaku followed with him stating; 'It's not like I'm a new player coming in, not knowing what to expect. I've scored a fair amount of goals here but the past is the past. Now I'm a new version of that player from before. I've evolved and now we have to challenge for the Premier League'.

On Tuesday 17th August we said goodbye to Tammy Abraham who joined Jose Mourinho at Roma for a fee of around £34m with an option to buy-back from June 2023. I personally liked Tammy, an academy player who gave everything for the club. He always came across as a true professional with a good attitude. I don't think any Chelsea fan felt he was the finished article but at 23 years old not many strikers are. I think many supporters felt we might see him back at Stamford Bridge one day. Tammy posted this on his Intagram account; "Thank you - it's time to say goodbye to a club that means so much to me and my family. From playing at the academy as a young kid from Peckham to winning the Champions League all those years later. I want to say thank you to my team mates, The Academy, all the staff and of course, the Chelsea fans who have always supported me. Wouldn't be who I am today without you guys. Bring me more trophies home boys! Love you all x TA9 out."

The next day the club held an open training session at Stamford Bridge where 2,000 fans had the opportunity to watch the team train from the West Stand Lower. Those fans were treated to Azpilicueta and Jorginho parading the Champions League trophy and Super Cup with the squad and heard a question and answer with manager Thomas Tuchel and Chelsea's new number nine, Romelu Lukaku.

Both Michy Batshyuai (Besiktas) and Kenedy (Flamengo) signed contract extensions but were loaned for the coming season.

22nd August
Premier League
Arsenal 0-2 Chelsea
Emirates Stadium
Attendance: 58,729

Chelsea (4-2-3-1): Mendy, Azpilicueta (c), Christensen, Rudiger, James, Jorginho, Kovacic (Kante 72), Alonso, Mount (Ziyech 82), Lukaku, Havertz (Werner 90)
Chelsea Goals: Lukaku (15), James (35)

Arsenal (4-2-3-1): Leno, Soares, Holding, Mari, Tierney (Tavares 66), Lokonga, Xhaka (c), Pepe, Smith Rowe, Saka (Aubameyang 61), Martinelli (Balogun 79)

Preparation going into the London derby was very positive, Jorginho and N'Golo Kante had been nominated for UEFA Player Of The Year along with Kevin De Bruyne and Thomas Tuchel had been nominated for UEFA Coach Of The Year alongside Pep Guardiola. Chelsea's Emma Hayes was also on the shortlist for Women's Coach Of The Year.

Emerson Palmieri moved to Lyon on loan for the season and Thomas Tuchel confirmed Trevoh Chalobah would remain with the first team squad for the season. Tickets for the game inevitably sold out very quickly with 2,873 blues in attendance. Arsenal on the other hand were struggling to sell out their first game back. It was apparent on social media that this was an issue and they couldn't put them on general sale, for fear that Chelsea fans would end up being in the home ends, which often used to happen in the 80's and 90's.

Christian Pulisic missed the game after testing positive for Covid-19 as did Arsenal's Willian and Ben White. Three weeks after beating Arsenal at the Emirates in the MIND Series it was a much different line-up. Most notable was Romelu Lukaku going straight into the team and making his second debut. Thomas Tuchel said pre-match 'We signed him to play... we didn't sign him to come off the bench'.

The whole game it felt Chelsea didn't really have to get out of second gear. Arsenal had a few chances but never really threatened and neither did I feel uncomfortable that we wouldn't win. Even when Arsenal are at their lowest they've tended to always put in a top performance against us but this game was different. We were always in control and should have scored more goals.

Romelu Lukaku opened the scoring within just 15 minutes. An easy tap-in but it was he who started the move, a pass to Kovacic who found Reece James on the right wing who crossed perfectly and Romelu couldn't miss after fending off Mari. It was so noticeable Lukaku's physical presence throughout the game holding up play and creating space for other players.

Reece James made it 2-0 ten minutes before half-time with a thunderous shot into the top corner after some great play from Havertz, Alonso and Mount.

Lukaku hit the crossbar in the second-half after a good save and despite James getting a goal and an assist it was Rom's day and it was he who was awarded Man Of The Match and was serenaded throughout by the 'Champions Of Europe' section at the Emirates. A mention to captain Cesar Azpilicueta who defensively was superb throughout. Two wins from two London derbies now, without a goal conceded. Next up, Liverpool away.

Leading up to the Liverpool game there were further departures as the transfer deadline edged ever closer. Davide Zapacosta joined Atalanta on a permanent deal and youngster Ike Ugo also left permanently joining Genk. Baba Rahman extended his Chelsea contract before moving on loan to Championship club Reading.

After the conclusion of the Carabao Cup second round, the third round draw was made. All the Premier League clubs invloved in European competitions entered the draw at this stage. Chelsea would face Aston Villa at Stamford Bridge.

Two days before the trip to Anfield there was the UEFA 2020/21 awards with much Chelsea involvement, hosted by none other than Michael Essien and Branislav Ivanovic.

Thomas Tuchel – Men's Coach Of The Year

Jorginho – UEFA Men's Player Of The Year
Edouard Mendy – Champions League Goalkeeper Of The Year
N'Golo Kante – Champions League Midfielder Of The Year
On the same day the Champions League group stage draw was made and Chelsea would face Juventus, Zenit St. Petersburg and Malmo in Group H.

28th August
Premier League
Liverpool 1-1 Chelsea
Anfield
Attendance: 53,100

Chelsea (3-4-3): Mendy, Azpilicueta (c), Christensen, Rudiger, James, Jorginho (Chalobah 88), Kante (Kovacic h-t) , Alonso, Havertz (Thiago Silva h-t), Lukaku, Mount
Chelsea Goal: Havertz (21)

Liverpool (4-3-3): Alisson, Alexander-Arnold, Matip, Van Dijk, Robertson (Tsimikas 86), Henderson (c) (Thiago 73), Fabinho, Elliot, Mane, Firmino (Jota 43), Salah
Liverpool Goal: Salah (45 Pen)

There was a lot going on at the club as we built up to the match. Chelsea released the new third kit which like always had split opinions. Chelsea would continue to be in blue for the game and the away allocation of 2,887 sold out instantly despite the difficulty of supporters getting home after a 5:30pm kick-off. Most notable was captain Cesar Azpilicueta making his 300th Premier League appearance on his 32nd birthday.

Both teams went into the match winning their first two games so it was all set up to be an early season cracker. Chelsea had the better early chances and took the lead on 21 minutes with a superb looping header from Kai Havertz after Reece James had delivered a great corner.

The game changed in dramatic controversial circumstances shortly before half-time with Reece James being sent off after a

VAR review. Referee Anthony Taylor looked at his monitor and quickly made the decision which also resulted in a penalty. It seemed harsh in all honesty and the ball had come off Reece' knee before hitting his hand with Taylor only seeing a still frame of the incident before making his decision. Mohammed Salah converted the penalty and more controversy followed as Mendy kicked the ball away shortly after causing a confrontation between both sets of players. Chelsea clearly aggrieved and so was Thomas Tuchel. Both Edouard Mendy and Antonio Rudiger were booked. It was an extremely frustrating end to the first-half especially when we had chances to make it 2-0.

At half-time there's no doubt we'd all have been over the moon if we could hold on and we did just that. We were defensively solid, organised and limited Liverpool to very few chances. A terrific point in the circumstances and Andreas Christensen deservedly being awarded Man Of The Match.

The first international break was now upon us but there was a few more transfers to be decided before deadline day. Further loans for Danny Drinkwater, Tiemoue Bakayoko, Dujon Sterling and Ethan Ampadu. Most notable was the permanent departure of Kurt Zouma. A fee close to £30m saw Kurt move across London to West Ham.

Kurt posted on his Instagram account:

"It has been a huge honour to be part of the success of this amazing club! The journey has been full of emotions.. I'll never be thankful enough @chelseafc see you soon!"

On transfer deadline day Chelsea were still trying to buy centre back Jules Kounde from Sevilla but a fee could not be agreed. However, a loan deal for Atletico Madrid midfielder Saul Niguez went through just before the 11pm deadline. There was also an option to buy at the end of the season.

It was a truly remarkable transfer window and one of the most memorable to date. Jack Grealish to Manchester City was a British record at £100m, Harry Kane stayed at Tottenham, Lionel Messi Joined PSG, Antoine Griezmann rejoined Atletico Madrid and Cristiano Ronaldo rejoined Manchester United.

SEPTEMBER 2021

For Chelsea it appeared a very positive window as we strengthened in an area that needed addressing and players were loaned-out and sold. Quality was needed, not quantity.

There was now a two week international break before we faced Aston Villa at Stamford Bridge in the Premier League. Frustrating as we were only three league games into the new season. During the break the club announced that with the number of tickets sold and those who bought the live streams for the MIND (pre-season) Series supporters of Chelsea, Arsenal and Tottenham raised £228,064.08. A fantastic amount raising money for a great mental health charity.

Reece James would face a one game ban for his red card at Liverpool and the club were fined £25,000 for 'failing to control their players' as a result of the aftermath. However, there were no repercussions for referee Anthony Taylor after another poor and controversial display involving a Chelsea match.

Japan withdrew themselves as the host nation for the FIFA Club World Cup with it due to take place in the December over COVID-19 concerns. During this time an alternative was being arranged.

Shortly after the transfer window shut clubs had to submit their completed squad to the Premier League.

Chelsea; Arrizabalaga, Rudiger, Alonso, Christensen, Jorginho, Thiago Silva, Kante, Kovacic, Lukaku, Pulisic, Werner, Loftus-Cheek, Bettinelli, Chalobah, Mendy, Niguez, Barkley, Mount, Hudson-Odoi, Chilwell, Ziyech, James, Azpilicueta, Havertz, Sarr, Baker, Bergstrom

11ᵗʰ September
Premier League
Chelsea 3-0 Aston Villa
Stamford Bridge
Attendance: 39,969

Chelsea (3-4-3): Mendy, Chalobah, Thiago Silva, Rudiger, Hudson-Odoi (Werner 82), Kovacic, Saul (Jorginho h-t), Alonso (c), Ziyech, Lukaku, Havertz (Azpilicueta 64)
Chelsea Goals: Lukaku (15, 90), Kovacic (49)

Aston Villa (3-5-2): Steer, Tuanzebe, Konsa, Mings, Cash, Luiz (Nakamba 79), McGinn, Ramsey (Bailey 56), Targett, Ings (Traore 69), Watkins

September 11ᵗʰ, a day no one will ever forget. The Aston Villa game marked 20 years since that tragic day, we'll never forget all those that perished in New York.

My dad couldn't make the game so my brother Steve took his ticket, he doesn't go too regularly but when he does he always wants to make the most of it! Despite it being a 5:30pm kick-off it was always going to be an early meet up. Firstly I met with Mark Worrall at the 'cfcuk' stall opposite Fulham Broadway station for a catch up and sign some copies of my book 'Blue Days'.

It was then onto the Pizza Express further down the Fulham Road near the Chelsea and Westminster Hospital. Why am I telling you this you ask? When we were kids in the 80's and early 90's this is where we always used to go for lunch before a game with our dad (Rick) and friends. It's just like any other restaurant but it holds many memories, as does the walk to Stamford Bridge from the other direction. We had some food and drinks before making our way to the Chelsea Pensioner pub. By 3pm there was a huge queue so we decided to have a couple of drinks in Kona Kai (we remember it as The Britannia). It was also buzzing in there as we watched the other scores come through on Sky's Soccer Saturday. Kick-off was edging closer and news of the team spread around the pub. In all honesty I was a little surprised by the line-up and thought we may be underestimating Aston Villa. With Pulisic and Kante injured Tuchel also left out Azpilicueta, Jorginho and Mason Mount. However, there was a lot of games to come in a short space of time. Saul Niguez made his debut with Lukaku making his second Stamford Bridge debut. Callum Hudson-Odoi was making his 100th appearance for The Blues, Jorginho making his 100th Premier League appearance and Marcos Alonso was made captain in the absence of Cesar. Thiago Silva also came back into the team at the last minute as his national team Brazil were asking FIFA to suspend eight players from playing due to Covid-19 quarantine protocols.

Once inside Stamford Bridge it was a terrific atmosphere and made even better with a huge Mason Mount flag covering the entire Matthew Harding Lower stand. An image of Mason with the Champions League stating 'The Boy Who Had A Dream'.

The game itself was extremely open with both teams having chances. It was the main man Romelu Lukaku who opened the scoring after 15 minutes. A tremendous through ball from Matteo Kovacic which allowed Lukaku to cut inside the defender before hitting his shot hard and low through the goalkeeper. At half-time much discussion was that we were obviously pleased with the score line but felt we were riding our luck at times. Saul Niguez had a very difficult debut getting used to the pace of the game and was caught in possession a number of times. He was substituted with Jorginho coming on.

The nerves were quickly settled in the second-half as Kovacic scored his first goal at Stamford Bridge. A short backpass from Tyrone Mings allowed Kovacic to pounce and he cleverly lifted the ball over the outrushing Steer in goal. 2-0!

On the 58th minute there was a wonderful tribute to comedian and season ticket holder Sean Lock who sadly passed away. The whole of Stamford Bridge were on their feet clapping in appreciation. There was also some lovely words from Johnny Vaughan in the match day programme.

The game was sealed in injury time with some great work from substitute Cesar Azpilicueta on the right hand side. He found Lukaku on the edge of the box who rifled the ball in to the top corner. "Ro-me, Ro-me-lu, Romelu Lukaku".

It was a great win and Lukaku was clinical, something we'd missed in previous seasons. Two shots on goal from the Belgian and two great goals. Kovacic most probably played his best game in a Chelsea shirt, Jorghino settled the team in the second-half and nothing was going to get past Mendy and Thiago Silva who were both exceptional. The win was Chelsea's 600th in the Premier League and we were now the second team to do this, behind only Manchester United.

Me and Steve headed straight to the Chelsea Pensioner pub after the game where the celebrations carried on late into the night. We just never stopped singing, by the time we got back to Fulham Broadway station I was starting to lose my voice. There was however time for "one for the road". A quick one in the Wetherspoons and to wish @terrykomatsu a very happy birthday.

A great day all round with Zenit St Petersburg to come on the Tuesday as we started our Champions League defence at Stamford Bridge.

14th September
Champions League, Group H, Match Day 1
Chelsea 1-0 Zenit St Petersburg
Stamford Bridge
Attendance: 39,525

Chelsea (3-4-3): Mendy, Azpilicueta (c) (Thiago Silva 82), Christensen, Rudiger, James, Kovacic, Jorginho, Alonso (Chilwell 82), Ziyech (Havertz 63), Lukaku, Mount (Loftus-Cheek 90)
Chelsea Goal: Lukaku (69)

Zenit St Petersburg (5-4-1): Kritsyuk, Sutormin, Barrios, Chistiakov, Rakitskyy (Krugovoi 88), Santos (c), Malcom (Dzyuba 76), Kuzyaev (Kravtsov 82), Wendel (Erokhin 76), Claudinho (Mostovoy 88), Azmoun

108 days since that magical night in Porto we kicked off the defence of our Champions League trophy playing Zenit St

Petersburg for the first time in our history. Edouard Mendy was making his 50th Chelsea appearance with captain Cesar Azpilicueta making his 50th Champions League appearance. Before the game Thomas Tuchel, Edouard Mendy, Jorginho and N'Golo Kante were presented with their deserved individual UEFA awards.

European nights at Stamford Bridge have always been special and the firework display before the match was very impressive. Unfortunately there wasn't too many fireworks on the pitch. Zenit were organised and chances were few and far between for both teams.

The breakthrough goal finally happened with 20 minutes remaining. A wonderful cross into the box from Azpilicueta found Lukaku who towered above defenders to head home. A great goal but also a huge sigh of relief. It finished 1-0 and although it was far from a classic it was important to win the first game in the group. Lukaku had now scored four goals in four games.

Unfortunately during the game Reece James' house was broken into with a safe stolen which contained his Champions League and Super Cup Winners medals.

19th September
Premier League
Tottenham Hotspur 0-3 Chelsea
White Hart Lane
Attendance: 60,059

Chelsea (3-4-2-1): Kepa, Christensen, Thiago Silva, Rudiger, Azpilicueta (c), Jorginho, Kovacic, Alonso, Mount (Kante h-t), Havertz (Werner 70), Lukaku
Chelsea Goals: Thiago Silva (49), Kante (57), Rudiger (90)

Tottenham Hotspur (4-3-3): Lloris (c), Royal, Romero (Sanchez 83), Dier, Reguilon, Ndombele (Skipp 62), Hojbjerg, Alli, Lo Celso (Gil 62), Son, Kane

Always a big game against Tottenham, and this one was no

different. The morning of the game the news broke that Jimmy Greaves had sadly passed away aged 81. A legend of both clubs with a minutes applause taking place before the game and players wearing black arm bands as a mark of respect.

Most notable team news was the absence of Mendy who didn't recover in time after an injury against Zenit with Kepa replacing him. Alonso was still favoured over Chilwell on the left side and there was a return to the bench for N'Golo Kante.

Tottenham started the game better than Chelsea although there wasn't too many chances to speak of. It was apparent that Mount, Havertz and Lukaku were all struggling to get into the game. With the score 0-0 at half-time it wasn't all doom and gloom but improvements were certainly needed if we were to take all three points.

Kante replaced Mount and the game completely changed. He was simply exceptional! Thiago Silva opened the scoring shortly after the re-start with a great header from Marcos Alonso' out swinging corner. Just eight minutes later it was 2-0 and Kante scored a rare goal from outside box after his shot took a big deflection off Dier and trickled over the line after coming off the post.

Chelsea were very much in control and had many other second-half chances from Kovacic, Thiago Silva, Alonso and Lukaku. It was pure dominance and Antonio Rudiger scored the final goal in the last minute sweeping the ball in after a clever cut back from substitute Timo Werner. It was a terrific second-half performance with the Chelsea fans in full voice throughout. Thiago Silva was Man Of The Match but there were also some other great performances from the likes of Kante, Rudiger, Alonso and Kovacic. Chelsea had now won all three of the league games played at the new White Hart Lane without conceding a goal. Six games now played with Chelsea joint top of the league with Manchester United. A very positive start, having already played Tottenham, Liverpool and Arsenal away from home.

22nd September
Carabao Cup 3rd Round

Chelsea 1-1 Aston Villa (Chelsea won 4-3 on penalties)
Stamford Bridge
Attendance: 35,892

Chelsea (3-5-2): Kepa, James, Chalobah, Sarr, Hudson-Odoi, Kante (c) (Mount h-t), Loftus-Cheek, Saul (Barkley 76), Chilwell, Ziyech (Lukaku 76), Werner
Chelsea Goal: Werner (54)

Aston Villa (4-4-2): Steer, Cash (Konsa 76), Tuanzebe, Hause, Young (c), Sanson (Carney 42), Nakamba, Traore (Philogene–Bidace 63), Buendia, El Ghazi, Archer
Aston Villa Goal: Archer (64)

The games were coming very quickly and now attention turned to the Carabao Cup and Aston Villa. Although we had faced them in 2006 in the same competition it was a game in 1998 that instantly came to mind when the draw was made. A 4-1 Chelsea victory that saw a hat trick from Gianluca Viall, a red card for Dennis Wise and a debut for John Terry.

I initially didn't plan on going to this one and decided not to buy tickets. However, a few days before the game I was contacted by sponsors '3' and was offered a complimentary ticket in the new Westview.

Despite domestic trophies not being at the top of the priority list I've always liked them with the League Cup and F.A Cup giving us some great memories. I particularly enjoyed the wins in 2005 and 2007 at the Millennium Stadium in Cardiff when Wembley was being redeveloped.

Once work was done it was straight down to Stamford Bridge to pick up my ticket from the Millennium suite. However first it would be a few pints in the Cock Tavern pub and catching up with the likes of @carefreecammy amongst others. The atmosphere was building as we awaited team news. It was always inevitable the team selection would be very different to recent games and the fringe players would get an opportunity to impress Thomas Tuchel. Most notable was a start for Ruben Loftus-Cheek, a great talent who has been so unfortunate with injuries. There was also a debut for defender Malang Sarr.

It took a while to get in the ground with queues seeming longer than usual, no doubt due to paper tickets and Covid-19 checks. I made it into my seat just before the minute's applause for Jimmy Greaves which was a sombre moment. I have to say I was impressed with the 'Westview' with my seat just left of the halfway line. A near full attendance at Stamford Bridge with a decent atmosphere for a League Cup tie. The game wasn't a classic and in all honesty I didn't expect it to be. Chances for both sides in the first-half but the best opportunity fell to Aston Villa with Kepa making a fine one on one save and Reece James clearing off the line from the rebound.

Mason Mount replaced N'Golo Kante at half-time and took the captain's armband and the opening goal came soon after the re-start. A terrific cross from Reece James found Timo Werner who rose above the Villa defence to head in. A decent goal that sparked the tie into life. I thought at this stage Chelsea would go on to dominate the match but that wasn't the case with Villa equalising ten minutes later through Archer with a very good header. Romelu Lukaku and Ross Barkley came on later in the second-half but we couldn't find a way through. With no extra-time it was straight to a penalty shoot out.

Penalties were to be taken towards the Matthew Harding stand with Aston Villa to take first. El Ghazi scored but so did Lukaku, Ashley Young stepped up to the sound of boo's and jeers as he rattled the crossbar to the delight behind the goal. Mason Mount sent the goalkeeper the wrong way and Kepa saved brilliantly from Nakamba. Barkley made it 3-1 with Chelsea very much in control and despite Konsa making it 3-2 Chilwell had the chance to put us through to the fourth round. He also rattled the crossbar and it was now down to Reece James to win it after Buendia sent Kepa the wrong way. Reece stepped up and fired into the top left-hand corner. A great winning penalty and a huge sigh of relief.

There was some very good individual performances from the likes of Loftus-Cheek, Kepa, James, Werner and Chalobah. On the tube at Earl's Court I finally got a phone signal and it flashed up that The Blues would play Southampton in round four at Stamford Bridge.

25th September
Premier League
Chelsea 0-1 Manchester City
Stamford Bridge
Attendance: 40,036

Chelsea (3-5-2): Mendy, Azpilicueta (c), Christensen, Rudiger, James (Thiago Silva 29), Kante (Havertz 60), Jorginho (Loftus-Cheek 76), Kovacic, Alonso, Lukaku, Werner

Manchester City (3-5-2): Edison, Walker, Dias (c), Laporte, Cancelo, Rodri, Silva, De Bryne (Mahrez 80), Jesus, Foden (Fernandinho 87), Grealish (Sterling 87)
Manchester City Goal: Jesus (53)

September 25th is a date I'll personally never forget. This game marked 28 years since I was the Chelsea mascot against Liverpool. A 1-0 victory with Neil Shipperley scoring the winner. One of those Chelsea memories that'll stay with me, leading the team out and meeting my heroes.

It was the early Saturday lunchtime kick-off and it was always going to be a hard game. As the country was going into unnecessary panic over petrol I was more than happy to go by train despite a few delays. It was also the first time in 18 months that I was back sat next to my dad. It was a game neither of us wanted to miss and it was all set to be a game full of quality and Stamford Bridge to remind Manchester City supporters exactly 'what we are', Champions Of Europe.

I managed to squeeze in a quick pint in the Cock Tavern before the game and bumping into many of the usual suspects. The atmosphere was building despite the early start and confidence was high going into the match. The team news broke with no surprises, just the formation, and despite Kepa doing very well since coming into the team it was good to have Mendy back in goal. On arrival next to the programme sellers there was already a bad omen entering Stamford Bridge as club sponsors Zapp were giving out free scarves to supporters. You might think this was a nice gesture but they were in the colours of opponents Manchester City. Once inside the ground 'The Shed End' unveiled a Champions League trophy flag in the upper tier reminding the travelling Manchester City fans located to the right.

In all honesty it was probably the worst performance I can remember under Thomas Tuchel to date. From minute one we weren't in the game and Manchester City were dominant throughout. There was no bridge between the midfield and Werner and Lukaku who were often left isolated feeding off scraps. We managed to get to half-time at 0-0 by only having 33% of the possession. Manchester City deservedly took the lead shortly after half-time through Jesus after a clever turn and although we improved we never really created anything. If it wasn't for Edouard Mendy, Thiago Silva, Antonio Rudiger and Andreas Christensen it would have been a lot worse.

A cameo for Ruben Loftus-Cheek, who really did impress, was the only positive for Chelsea, but it was apparent we missed Mason Mount who was out injured. Sometimes you get games like this and tactically Pep Guardiola got this one right. It was always going to be a difficult game but not having one shot on target was very frustrating. It wasn't all doom and gloom as Manchester United lost at home to Aston Villa, Tottenham lost the North London derby and Liverpool dropped points at Brentford. Chelsea were now third after six games on 13 points which on reflection was still very positive considering the difficult run of fixtures we started with.

29th September
Champions League, Group H, Match Day 2
Juventus 1-0 Chelsea
Allianz Stadium, Turin
Attendance: 19,934

Chelsea (3-4-3): Mendy, Christensen (Barkley 75), Thiago Silva, Rudiger, Azpilicueta (c) (Loftus-Cheek 62), Jorginho (Chalobah 62), Kovacic, Alonso (Chiwell h-t), Havertz, Lukaku, Ziyech (Hudson-Odoi 62)

Juventus (4-4-2): Szczesny, Danilo, Bonucci (c), De Ligt, Sandro, Cuadrado, Bentancur (Chiellini 83), Locatelli, Rabiot (McKennie 76), Bernardeschi (Kulusevski 65), Chiesa (Kean 76)
Juventus Goal: Chiesa (46)

Thomas Tuchel announced that Mason Mount and Christian Pulisic were still unavailable and Reece James had not recovered from his injury sustained against Manchester City which forced him off during the game. N'Golo Kante was also ruled out due to testing positive for Covid-19.

September 29th marked 50 years since Chelsea beat Jeunesse Hautcharage 13-0 at Stamford Bridge in the European Cup Winners' Cup first round, second-leg. An aggregate 21-0 score line with Peter Osgood scoring eight goals over both legs. It still remains the biggest score line in European football history.

A new song emerged from Chelsea fans who travelled to Turin which was sung in bars leading up to kick-off.

"Mount played in Kai, Today was his day, He rounded the keeper, To put it away, So fuck your blue moon, and be on your way, Stop crying Man City." (To the tune of 'Stop Crying Your Heart Out' – Oasis)

Looking to bounce back quickly from the Manchester City game it was unfortunately more of the same with another lacklustre performance. We had much of the ball in the first-half but only managed one shot on target from Romelu Lukaku.

Thinking we would come out much better in the second-half to our disbelief we found ourselves 1-0 down after just ten seconds with a very good goal from Federico Chiesa. It could easily have been 2-0 if not for wasteful finishing.

Lukaku had another chance late on as did Kai Havertz but neither were able to test the goalkeeper. Ross Barkley, Callum Hudson-Odoi, Ruben Loftus-Cheek and Trevoh Chalobah all came on later in the second-half but we couldn't find an equaliser. Despite losing two games on the bounce against good opposition we hadn't played well. Southampton in the Premier League now became a much bigger game.

Leading up to the match the international squads were announced which saw Mason Mount and Reece James included in the England squad, as well as former blue Fikayo Tomori who was continuing to impress at AC Milan.

This was clearly to the surprise of Thomas Tuchel, as when he was asked about Reece James in his press conference he said, "Maybe Reece goes with the water polo team because right now he trains in the pool".

Crystal Palace announced that Chelsea loanee Conor Gallagher had been voted as their Player Of The Month for September. He also won the award in August!

OCTOBER 2021

2nd October
Premier League
Chelsea 3-1 Southampton
Stamford Bridge
Attendance: 40,109

Chelsea (3-4-3): Mendy, Chalobah, Thiago Silva, Rudiger, Azpilicueta (c), Loftus-Cheek (Barkley 83), Kovacic (Jorginho 73), Chilwell, Hudson-Odoi (Mount 65), Lukaku, Werner
Chelsea Goals: Chalobah (9), Werner (84), Chilwell (89)

Southampton (4-4-2): McCarthy, Livramento, Salisu, Bednarek, Walker-Peters, Walcott (Diallo h-t), Romeu, Ward-Prowse, Tella (Djenepo 73), Redmond, Armstrong
Southampton Goal: Ward-Prowse (61 pen)

It was vital we got back to winning ways before another international break and put an end to what some of the press were describing 'a mini crisis' despite it being only two 1-0 defeats. Southampton were yet to win a league game but you could certainly feel the tension before this one. I'm quite a tradionalist so I always like a Saturday 3pm kick-off. However, it rained and rained and rained.

A minutes applause was held just before kick-off for England 1966 World Cup winner Roger Hunt who passed away leading up to this round of Premier League fixtures.

The perfect start saw Chelsea 1-0 up after just nine minutes. A corner from Ben Chilwell was glanced on by the impressive Ruben Loftus-Cheek and Trevoh Chalobah was there at the far post who finished with a diving header. Chelsea had other chances to double the lead and there was also a let off where Theo Walcott should've done better with a glancing header. It was shortly before half-time where the drama really happened. Some great play from Hudson-Odoi on the left who crossed for Timo Werner, he headed in to the delight of the Shed End. To everyone's surprise there was a VAR check and referee Martin Atkinson went over to the pitch side monitor. The goal was disallowed as Azpilicueta was adjudged to have fouled Walker-Peters in the build-up. A ridiculous decision as there had been many patterns of play after the alleged foul took place. One of my biggest gripes about VAR is how far back do you have to go? Everyone was rightly fuming, Thomas Tuchel even received a yellow card for his protest. Just for the record there was absolutely no mention of this incident later that night on Match Of The Day.

Chelsea started the second-half on the front foot but it was Southampton that equalised from the spot on the hour mark through James Ward-Prowse. A poor challenge from Ben Chilwell on former blue Tino Livramento gave Atkinson no choice.

Werner had a great chance to put Chelsea back in the lead after some great skill from Lukaku but it was well saved from McCarthy. Another VAR controversy saw James Ward-Prowse sent off after a challenge on Jorginho which I didn't feel was clear and obvious.

Ross Barkley came on for Loftus-Cheek and it was he who produced a fantastic ball to Azpilicueta who played in Werner to score. A fantastic moment that he most definitely deserved. There was no way back for Southampton now as we approached 90 minutes, there was time for another Chelsea goal. Lukaku hit the post from close-range and then so did Azpilicueta with the ball eventually falling to Chilwell who rifled a shot goal wards, it had just crossed the line, though most supporters thought goal keeper McCarthy had kept it out. A hard fought victory but a much-needed and deserved one.

Timo Werner stated after the game; "My first goal which was disallowed was a little bit like the story of my whole Chelsea career in one game".

At this point incredibly Timo Werner now had 16 goals disallowed by VAR since he arrived. Chelsea now had 12 different goal scorers in seven Premier League games. We went into the second international break one point clear at the top of the table.

The biggest news during the international break was undoubtedly the Saudi Arabian takeover of Newcastle United which was confirmed on Wednesday 7th October. Chelsea would be heading to the North East to face Newcastle at the end of the month with tickets selling out to season ticket holders in a matter of minutes.

The next day the Ballon d'Or shortlist was announced. Cesar Azpilicueta, Jorginho, N'Golo Kante, Mason Mount and Romelu Lukaku were all included in the final 30.

France won the Nations League defeating Spain 2-1 in the Final.

16th October
Premier League
Brentford 0-1 Chelsea
Brentford Community Stadium
Attendance: 16,940

Chelsea (3-5-2): Mendy, Chalobah, Christensen, Sarr, Azpilicueta (c) (James 89), Kante, Loftus-Cheek, Kovacic (Mount 65), Chilwell, Werner, Lukaku (Havertz 77)
Chelsea Goal: Chilwell (45)

Brentford (3-5-2): Raya, Zanka, Pinnock, Jansson (c), Canos (Ghoddos 72), Jensen, Norgaard, Onyeka (Forss 67), Henry, Mbeumo, Toney

Brentford had a very good start to life in the Premier League and had already beaten Arsenal, West Ham and scored three against Liverpool. This had a potential banana skin written all over it and that was clear with SKY making it the 5:30pm kick-off. This was always going to be a difficult game after an international break and it wasn't helped with Anthony Taylor being appointed the referee after 80,000 Chelsea supporters had signed an online petition to have him banned from refereeing Chelsea games. Antonio Rudiger missed out through injury and Thiago Silva had to quarantine after being on international duty with Brazil.

Going into the game I wasn't too fussed with a big performance as long as we came away with three points and finished the weekend top of the league. To much surprise Malang Sarr made his Premier League debut and started in the back three with Christensen and Chalobah. Kante was also back in the team after recovering from Covid-19.

We started the game very positively and certainly took the sting out of the atmosphere. We restricted Brentford to very few chances despite one of them hitting the post. Lukaku thought he had put us 1-0 up after Werner crossed but it was adjudged offside. We did however made our dominance count on the stroke of half-time through an excellent half volley from Ben Chilwell. It was now three in three for Ben having scored against Southampton and for England during the international break.

Later in the second-half was a completely different story, like everyone else I was literally just waiting for Brentford to score. Sarr, Christensen and Chalobah stood strong in defensive duties but the Man Of The Match was undoubtedly Edouard Mendy. A truly superb performance making a number of top class saves and one he tipped onto the bar in the dying seconds. We didn't create much in the game but managed to hold on to what was a valuable three points. There was also another promising performance from Ruben Loftus-Cheek.

20th October
Champions League, Group H, Match Day 3
Chelsea 4-0 Malmo
Stamford Bridge
Attendance: 39,095

Chelsea (3-4-3): Mendy, Christensen, Thiago Silva, Rudiger, Azpilicueta (c), (James 65), Kante (Saul 65), Jorginho, Chilwell (Alonso 65), Mount, Lukaku (Havertz 23), Werner (Hudson-Odoi

44)

Chelsea Goals: Christensen (9), Jorginho (21 pen, 57 pen), Havertz (48)

Malmo (3-5-2): Dahlin (Diawara h-t), Larsson, Neilsen, Brorsson, Berget (Moisander 83), Pena (Rakip 58), Innocent, Christiansen (c) (Nalic 58), Olsson, Colak, Birmancevic (Abubakari h-t)

It was an eventful day and it started with Chelsea announcing a Limited Edition Champions of Europe shirt. Only 420 were made and it was named '42' to mark the minute Kai Havertz scored the winner in the Champions League final. It was basically the current home shirt with a lot of graffiti-type writing on it. Surprising considering it wasn't the shirt worn in Porto on that special night. It's an understatement to say it didn't go down well with supporters who were also less than impressed with the £195 price tag! Shortly before the match FIFA announced that the Club World Cup would take place in the United Arab Emirates early in the new year.

Christian Pulisic was the only player absent through injury and despite Thomas Tuchel stating in his pre-match press conference that Lukaku was mentally tired he started in attack. Many expected Hudson-Odoi to start but he was on the bench, there was a return for Thiago Silva and Jorginho.

The game was extremely straightforward, which was very welcomed amongst a very busy schedule. Andreas Christensen set us on our way finishing like a forward after just nine minutes. It wasn't long until we doubled our lead through a Jorginho penalty however it came at a cost. As a result of Lukaku being fouled he was forced to go off through injury and was replaced by Kai Havertz.

Approaching half-time and dominating the game there were more injury woes. This time Timo Werner went off with a hamstring problem and replaced by Callum Hudson-Odoi. Both substitutes linked up perfectly for the third goal shortly after half-time with Kai delicately lifting the ball over the outrushing goalkeeper after a perfect ball from Callum. The fourth and final goal came from another Jorginho penalty after Rudiger was fouled after a great run. Despite continued Chelsea dominance and more substitutions the game fizzled out. A great result on the night where it poured down with rain. The only disappointment was the injuries to Lukaku and Werner.

23rd October
Premier League
Chelsea 7-0 Norwich City
Stamford Bridge
Attendance: 40,113

Chelsea (3-4-3): Mendy, Chalobah, Thiago Silva, Rudiger, James, Jorginho (c) (Loftus-Cheek 62), Kovacic, Chilwell, Mount, Havertz (Barkley 70), Hudson-Odoi (Ziyech 70)
Chelsea Goals: Mount (7, 85 pen, 90), Hudson-Odoi (18), James (42), Chilwell (57), Aarons (og 62)

Norwich City (3-5-2): Krul, Kabak, Hanley (c), Gibson, Aarons, Lees-Melou (Rashica h-t), McLean, Normann, Giannoulis (Williams h-t), Pukki, Sargent (Omobamidele 69)

The day before the game marked 25 years since the tragic passing of Chelsea Vice Chairman and financial investor Matthew Harding. Some tributes were planned for the day of the Norwich game and although the club released a wonderful montage image of Matthew it was disappointing he wasn't the official programme cover feature.

It was the early Saturday kick-off which are often hard to get motivated for but it was top verses bottom and an expectation of seeing a few goals. The team certainly didn't disappoint. I went to the game with my brother Steve and once we arrived at Fulham Broadway we had a couple of early beers in the Cock Tavern. Team news filtered through with no real surprises given the injuries picked up against Malmo. Once inside Stamford Bridge there was an emotional minute's applause for Matthew Harding with chants of "There's only one Matthew Harding" ringing round the bridge with his crowd-surfer flag held aloft in the MHL.

It was complete Chelsea dominance from the very first whistle and it took just nine minutes for the deadlock to be broken. After some good work from Hudson-Odoi and Kovacic the ball was laid off to Mason Mount who hit a great shot from outside the box that nestled into the corner. Kovacic was again involved for the second goal when his defence-splitting ball found Hudson-Odoi who finished very well from the left-hand side. Approaching the break me and Steve were just about to go down for half-time beers, when Chelsea made it 3-0. Mount turned provider this time with a great ball to Reece James who lifted the ball over Tim Krul for a classy finish.

Norwich manager Daniel Farke made substitutions at half-time but in all honesty it didn't make any difference. However, early in the second-half Norwich had a great chance to pull one back after an out of character error from Ben Chilwell. Edouard Mendy came to his rescue with a fantastic block with his feet. It didn't take long for goal number four, with another great shot, this time from Chilwell who was in fine goal scoring form. Just five minutes later it was 5-0 with the goal being awarded to Norwich City's Max Aarons after some good work from Hudson-Odoi on the left-hand side. Things went from bad to worse for Norwich as they were reduced to ten men as Gibson received a second yellow card for a foul on Reece James.

More chances were created with Chelsea in full flow. Antonio Rudiger's shot was adjudged to be blocked by Normann's hand and after a long VAR review a penalty was awarded. Mason Mount stepped up and it was saved by Krul. Another VAR review determined that Krul stepped off his line and it would be retaken. Mason scored at the second attempt, it really was party time at Stamford Bridge. The Shed End were in full voice, ".....we're the middle.....we're the left side of The Shed".

Some great work from substitutes Ziyech and Loftus-Cheek before Ruben squared to Mason Mount who completed his hat trick in injury time.

A wonderful performance with the boys from Cobham contributing hugely in the seven goal thrashing and it was now 17 different goal scorers this season. Before going straight to the Chelsea Pensioner after the game we bumped into club legend Kerry Dixon and had a photo together.

We met up with @jonnysillitoe and a few of his friends who'd travelled down from Manchester on the day. The songs kept coming in the pub and so did the celebratory drinks. A top day and a performance, one Matthew Harding would've loved!

26th September
Carabao Cup 4th Round
Chelsea 1-1 Southampton (Chelsea won 4-3 on penalties)
Stamford Bridge
Attendance: 39,766

Chelsea (3-4-3): Kepa, James, Chalobah, Sarr, Hudson-Odoi, Kovacic, Saul, Alonso (c), Ziyech (Mount 67), Havertz, Barkley (Chilwell 67)
Chelsea Goal: Havertz (44)

Southampton (3-4-3): Forster, Valery, Lyanco. Salisu, Walker-Peters, S.Armstrong (c) (Smallbone 77), Diallo (Romeu 77), Djenepo (Livramento 83), Tella (Walcott 67), Adams (Long 66), A.Armstrong
Southampton Goal: Adams (47)

Attentions turned back to the Carabao Cup with Southampton visiting Stamford Bridge. Team changes were inevitable but this was far from a classic.

Southampton were impressive and so was the response to "Champions of Europe, we know what we are". Their travelling fans responded with "Johnstone's Paint Trophy, you'll never win that".
The breakthrough goal came just before half-time with a powerful header from Kai Havertz. Into the second-half and I felt we'd kick on after our goal. The complete opposite happened and it didn't

take long for Southampton to equalise through a scrappy goal from Che Adams. There were chances at both ends and if there was going to be a winner you felt it would be Southampton.

Similar to the previous round against Aston Villa the game would be decided with a penalty shootout at the Matthew Harding end. Armstrong scored then so did captain for the evening Marcos Alonso. Kepa saved Walcott's penalty on to the post but Forster went on to save from Mason Mount. Shane Long and Callum Hudson-Odoi both scored to make it 2-2 before Smallbone blasted over the bar. Chilwell and former blue Oriel Romeu scored so it would be Reece James once again to take the decisive penalty. Like the previous round he scored and Chelsea progressed to the quarter-final.

30th October
Premier League
Newcastle United 0-3 Chelsea
St Reece James' Park
Attendance: 52,209

Chelsea (3-4-3): Mendy, Christensen, Thiago Silva, Rudiger, James, Kante (Loftus-Cheek 64), Jorginho (c), Chilwell, Ziyech (Barkley 64), Havertz, Hudson-Odoi (Saul 88)
Chelsea Goals: James (65, 77), Jorginho (Pen 81)

Newcastle United (5-3-2): Darlow, Manquillo, Krafth, Lascelles (c), Clark, Ritchie, Hayden (Almiron 67), S. Longstaff (Shelvey 81), Fraser (Willock 67), Wilson, Saint-Maximin

Wow, wow, wow, what a day! I'm writing this heading home on the 6pm train from Newcastle Central Station to London Kings Cross.

Newcastle v Chelsea has been a significant fixture in my household ever since I met my wife Jo who is of course a Geordie. In all honesty she's not a huge football fan but it's naturally in the blood up there. Before our children came along we'd often visit her family in Newcastle and I'd try my best to coincide it with Chelsea playing Newcastle, Sunderland or Middlesbrough in the North

East.

When the fixtures were released in the summer I knew this particular game was scheduled during the half-term holiday and wondered if we could go up as a family. For one reason or another we ended up having family visiting us instead. Once the television games had been announced and our game at Newcastle remained a Saturday 3pm kick-off I thought I could still do this in a day. Anything other than that time is a nightmare for supporters to travel, so this was perfect.

Tickets went on sale to season ticket holders on the same day it was announced a Saudi Arabia takeover was imminent at St. James' Park. As it was a scramble for all season ticket holders I managed to get one although disappointed for many supporters who missed out. It was sold out in just a few minutes, with the demand so high I honestly felt we could have sold double the 3,227 allocation given. With the takeover now officially announced the next day the talk of Twitter was that Steve Bruce would eventually get sacked and it would be just our luck that Frank Lampard or Antonio Conte would be in the Newcastle hot seat just before we faced them. As we know Steve Bruce was sacked but it would be caretaker manager Graeme Jones in charge for the fixture.

Chelsea went into the game in fine form having thrashed Norwich 7-0 at Stamford Bridge the week before and progressing to the Carabao Cup quarter-final after defeating Southampton on penalties. Newcastle were still winless and we were hoping to extend our lead at the top of the table. Form goes out the window when we face the Magpies at St. James' Park where they usually turn into 1970 Brazil.

Setting the morning alarm for an away day is completely different from setting one for work, even if it means getting up earlier. Regardless of your age that buzz never leaves you, it's like being a kid again on Christmas morning. I was travelling from Essex with my first train at 7:30am so the alarm was set for 6:15am. Travelling into London that early on a Saturday morning usually consists of some people coming home from the night before. However, you also see other football fans all ready for a long trip. Once on the Hammersmith and City line there were groups of Ipswich fans travelling down to Plymouth and Millwall heading to Huddersfield.

Upon my arrival to Kings Cross there were a lot of Chelsea fans about eagerly awaiting the platform number for the 9:30am train. Although it was an early start I spare a thought for the fans who opted for the official supporters coach which departed Stamford Bridge at 6:30am. Once on the train many were trying to get a stream of the Carabao Cup quarter-final draw which was scheduled to take place on Soccer AM at 10:30am. Little did we know that the programme started at that time and the draw was at the end of the show. Chelsea drew Brentford away with fans instantly talking about what sort of allocation we'd get.

We arrived in Newcastle at 12:40 and it was inevitably straight to the pub. Coming out of the station you could already here the Chelsea fans belting out 'Champions of Europe, we know what we are' from the Victoria Comet pub across the road as fans spilt out onto the street. A nightmare to get in so I chose to have a drink in the Centurion bar at the station. A mix of Newcastle and Chelsea fans but a very good atmosphere. Bumped into a few of the usual suspects including fellow "cfcuk" fanzine contributor @carefreecammy. After a few drinks a group of around ten of us headed to the ground for a drink on the concourse.

Team news filtered through and most notably Mason Mount missed out through illness. A real blow as we were already missing Pulisic, Kovacic, Werner and Lukaku. It was then the famous trek up the 14 flights of stairs (140).

Chelsea fans were inevitably in full voice as the drinks were flowing. The noise continued into the ground with 'no noise from the Saudi boys'. The first-half in all honesty was quite a frustrating watch with plenty of possession but little penetration with only Ziyech coming close. The half-time carnage was in full effect despite not knowing if we'd have enough to take all three points. It was Ziyech again who nearly opened the scoring with a deflected shot hitting the post one minute into the second-half.

Reece James scored two fantastic goals in eight minutes that killed the game and sent us into a frenzy in the clouds. Jorginho put the cherry on the top of the cake from the spot after Havertz was brought down by Darlow. The atmosphere was superb throughout and the birth of the 'Super Tommy Tuchel.....' song which continued after the game, down the stairs and through the streets of Newcastle. The mood was made even better towards the end of the game as the news of Conor Gallagher scoring the winner at Manchester City and Liverpool dropping points at home to Brighton filtered through.

Back at Central Station it was the same faces on the train back to Kings Cross and I finally got home at 10pm, it was only then I noticed a large graze on my right shin. As a result of absolute 'limbs' when Reece scored but I couldn't tell you if it was for his first or second goal. The day finished off perfectly with 'Match Of The Day'.

NOVEMBER 2021

2nd November
Champions League, Group H, Match Day 4
Malmo 0-1 Chelsea
Eleda Stadion, Malmo
Attendance: 19,551

Chelsea (3-4-3): Mendy, Christensen, Thiago Silva, Rudiger, Azpilicueta (c), Loftus-Cheek, Jorginho, Alonso, Ziyech (Barkley 74), Havertz, Hudson-Odoi (Pulisic 74)
Chelsea Goal: Ziyech (56)

Malmo (3-5-2): Dahlin, Neilsen (c), Brorsson, Ahmedhodzic, Berget (Larsson 86), Pena (Lewicki 57), Innocent, Rieks (Olsson 57), Rakip (Birmancevic 86), Colak, Nanasi (Nalic 75)

On the day there wasn't much talk of the game even by Chelsea supporters. The talk was of former Chelsea manager Antonio Conte being announced as the new manager of Tottenham after the sacking of Nuno Espirito Santo. A sour one to take although there were mixed feelings and opinions on social media. I know it ended badly with him but I'll never forget the football we played in the 2016/17 season where we should have won the double. It is also inevitable that when you sack as many managers as Chelsea have they are likely to end up at a rival or a club you dislike at some point.

1,045 Chelsea fans made the trip to Sweden via Copenhagen with many literally heading over there a day or two after the trip to Newcastle. Squad rotation was inevitable for this game which saw both in-form Ben Chilwell and Reece James sit out. The match itself really wasn't a classic but we did enough to win 1-0 and edge closer to the knockout stages of the Champions League. In all fairness Malmo defended in numbers very well but Hakim Ziyech broke the deadlock early in the second-half after some great work on the wing from Callum Hudson-Odoi.

Ruben Loftus-Cheek had a fine game as did Jorginho who picked up the Man Of The Match award. It was also a great night for Christian Pulisic who returned to the team from injury and came on later in the second-half.

6th November
Premier League
Chelsea 1-1 Burnley
Stamford Bridge
Attendance: 39,798

Chelsea (3-4-3): Mendy, Christensen, Thiago Silva, Rudiger, James, Kante (Mount 85), Jorginho (c), Chilwell, Barkley (Loftus-Cheek 72), Hudson-Odoi (Pulisic 85), Havertz
Chelsea Goal: Havertz (34)

Burnley (4-4-2): Pope, Lowton, Tarkowski, Mee (c), Taylor, Gudmundsson (Vydra 70), Westwood, Brownhill, McNeil, Cornet (Pieters 88), Wood (Rodriguez 61)
Burnley Goal: Vydra (80)

After beating Norwich and Newcastle it was now for the third team in the bottom three for Chelsea to face. Confidence was very high and though knowing how well Sean Dyche can organise his team like many others I fully expected three points. Like always Chelsea acknowledged Remembrance Day perfectly with wreaths placed on the pitch and a huge crowd-surfer covering the Matthew Harding Lower stand stating 'Chelsea Remembers'. There was also a wonderful tribute on the front of the official match day programme.

The game itself was very frustrating and was reminiscent of league form from the season before. We deservedly took the lead in the first-half through a Kai Havertz header after a superb Reece James cross from the right hand side.

It was complete Chelsea dominance throughout the game with The Blues having 70% possession, 25 shots but only four on target. With many chances missed you always felt Burnley would get a chance and in the 80th minute they took it through Vydra. It was disappointing we couldn't go into the international break with a win but the blow was softened with West Ham beating Liverpool the next day.

On Monday 8th November Chelsea announced that along with Cardiff City, Manchester City, Manchester United and Tottenham, Safe Standing at Stamford Bridge would be introduced from January 2022. Managerial news was that both Daniel Farke and Dean Smith had been sacked from Norwich and Aston Villa and former Bournemouth boss Eddie Howe took over at Newcastle. Both Frank Lampard and John Terry were in contention for the jobs.

Mason Mount withdrew from the England squad after having his wisdom teeth removed and John Terry joined Twitter just in time to keep fans entertained during another international break.

20th November
Premier League
Leicester City 0-3 Chelsea
King Power Stadium
Attendance: 35,497

Chelsea (3-4-3): Mendy, Chalobah, Thiago Silva, Rudiger, James, Kante, Jorginho (c) (Loftus-Cheek 77) Chilwell, Mount (Ziyech 62), Havertz (Pulisic 62), Hudson-Odoi
Chelsea Goals: Rudiger (14), Kante (28), Pulisic 71)

Leicester City (3-4-3): Schmeichel (c), Amartey, Evans, Soyuncu, Albrighton, Ndidi, Soumare (Dewsbury-Hall 75), Castagne, Lookman (Iheanacho h-t), Vardy, Barnes (Maddison h-t)

Thomas Tuchel received the Manager Of The Month award for

October and Conor Gallagher was called up for the second England game away to San Marino. He made his debut in a 10-0 victory where qualification for the 2022 World Cup was secured.

Frank Lampard appeared all set to take the Norwich City job but turned it down after further talks. Dean Smith took the job and Steven Gerrard replaced him at Aston Villa after leaving Rangers. There was also uproar when Chelsea announced a huge increase in price for season ticket holders in the Westview for the 2022/23 season, appearing to price out loyal supporters to much disappointment.

Despite not taking our chances against Burnley the football on the pitch had been sensational at times. This continued.

We were the first game of the weekend with a 12:30pm kick-off at Leicester and a very early start for the 3,305 Chelsea fans who made the trip. They were in for an absolute treat with a dominant performance from start to finish in what many would've viewed as a potentially very difficult game. It really wasn't the case and that was apparent very early on with Ben Chilwell hitting the cross bar in the very early stages after a great ball from Jorginho. It wasn't long until we took the lead through a great Rudiger header from Chilwell's corner. He certainly loves scoring against them! It was then 2-0 close to the half hour mark with a wonderful individual goal through Kante. With no one making a challenge N'Golo just kept going and finished emphatically.

Into the second-half and despite continued Chelsea dominance Amartey had a great chance to pull one back but Mendy was equal to the shot and made a great save. Substitute Pulisic had a good chance to make it three but put the ball just went wide of the post. He did however get on the score sheet moments later from close-range after some good work from Hakim Ziyech. It finished 3-0 and it really was a fantastic performance and result. Our fans were again class throughout and it was nice to see our away kit make an appearance for the first time.

23rd November
Champions League, Group H, Match Day 5
Chelsea 4-0 Juventus

Stamford Bridge
Attendance: 39,513

Chelsea (3-4-3): Mendy, Chalobah, Thiago Silva, Rudiger, James, Kante (Loftus-Cheek 37), Jorginho (c) (Saul 76), Chilwell (Azpilicueta 71), Ziyech, Pulisic (Werner 71), Hudson-Odoi (Mount 76)
Chelsea Goals: Chalobah (25), James (56), Hudson-Odoi (58), Werner (90)

Juventus (4-4-2): Szczesny, Cuadrado (De Winter 80), Bonucci (c), De Ligt, Alex Sandro, McKennie, Bentancur (Dybala 59), Locatelli (Arthur 67), Rabiot, Morata (Kean 67), Chiesa (Kulusevski 80)

With Chelsea sitting second in the group and Juventus leading by three points this was a huge game. I was back at Stamford Bridge with my dad for this one and it was arguably the best performance of the season so far. It was Thomas Tuchel's 50th game in charge of The Blues and it was certainly one to remember. The atmosphere inside Stamford Bridge was electric with the usual 'Champions of Europe, we know what we are' ringing around the stadium. There were two changes from the win at Leicester with Hakim Ziyech starting and Christian Pulisic playing as the 'false 9'. Trevoh Chalobah opened the scoring on 25 minutes, lashing in emphatically from close-range after the ball dropped to him from a corner. Alvaro Morata was back at Stamford Bridge with the Chelsea faithful making their feelings perfectly clear towards the former blue. He had a wonderful chance to equalise in the first-half as he lifted the ball over the outrushing Mendy only for Thiago Silva to clear incredibly off the line. Shortly after, unfortunately Kante was replaced by Loftus-Cheek after being forced off by injury. In truth we should have been more than one goal up at half-time but speaking with my dad we both felt very confident going into the second-half.

Chelsea approached the second-half with such aggression and killed the game with two quick goals. The first through Reece

James who hit a ferocious shot on the half volley, this one finding the net after having one saved in the first-half. The next came just two minutes later finished superbly by Callum Hudson-Odoi after some great build-up play involving Ruben Loftus-Cheek. Stamford Bridge absolutely erupted with some great scenes of celebration from both players and fans. The sour note of the evening was an injury to Ben Chilwell which instantly seemed like a bad one. We had other chances in the match but the win was wrapped up in injury time thanks to substitute Timo Werner turning in Ziyech's low cross. We'd now go into our final group game away to Zenit St. Petersburg with first place in our hands.

It was certainly one of those special European nights under the lights at Stamford Bridge, a terrific team performance against one of the giants in world football. Chelsea had now scored 40 goals across all competitions with 15 of them coming from defenders.

28th November
Premier League
Chelsea 1-1 Manchester United
Stamford Bridge
Attendance: 40,041

Chelsea (3-4-3): Mendy, Chalobah, Thiago Silva, Rudiger, James, Loftus-Cheek, Jorginho (c), Alonso (Pulisic 78), Ziyech, Werner (Lukaku 82), Hudson-Odoi (Mount 78)
Chelsea Goal: Jorginho (69 pen)

Manchester United (4-3-3): De Gea, Wan-Bissaka, Lindelof, Bailly, Telles, McTominay, Matic, Fred, Sancho (Ronaldo 64), Fernandes (Van de Beek 88), Rashford (Lingard 77)
Manchester United Goal: Sancho (50)

Chelsea went into the match feeling very confident with some great performances. However losing Ben Chilwell to injury was a real blow who would be out for a lengthy time. For me personally it was a jam-packed Chelsea weekend, aslo doing the 'Legends

Stadium Tour' with Pat Nevin the day before. The Christmas tree and lights were up at Stamford Bridge and the weather was absolutely freezing with some parts of the country having snow. Pre-match was fantastic, a quick visit to the 'cfcuk' stall to see @gate17marco and @onlyapound before Paul Canoville stopped for a chat. Soon off to the Cock Tavern pub and meeting up with some old and new faces. Further drinks and a meal with my dad before heading to the ground.

The atmosphere was decent and that feel of another really big game. Most notable from the team news was Timo Werner was starting as the central striker and Marcos Alonso replaced the injured Chilwell at left wing-back. Michael Carrick in temporary charge of Manchester United after the sacking of Ole Gunnar Solsjaer had a very defensive set up with Cristiano Ronaldo on the bench. Before the kick-off Chelsea showed their support of the Rainbow Laces campaign promoting the equality campaign.

It was a very dominant display from Chelsea and we should have taken an early lead through Callum Hudson-Odoi who was denied by De Gea. Hakim Ziyech and Reece James had chances to score and Antonio Rudiger hit the cross bar with a great strike. In all honesty it was disappointing to go into half-time at 0-0. The second-half started similarly to the first. However, just five minutes in, Manchester United took the lead completely against the run of play. A Chelsea free kick was charged down and hoofed up field. Jorginho was the last man and failed to control the ball and Sancho was clear to run in on goal and score easily. Mistakes happen in football but it did surprise me one of centre backs didn't stay back as well.

Jorginho turned to hero with 20 minutes remaining after converting from the penalty spot after Thiago Silva had been fouled by Wan-Bissaka. He showed a lot of character to score the way he did. Further chances came from Hudson-Odoi, Ziyech and Werner but just couldn't convert. Thomas Tuchel was booked in injury time for his reaction for substitiute Ronaldo not being flagged for offside, everyone could tell he was. There was still time for a last gasp chance and it fell to Rudiger inside the box but his shot landed well over the cross bar. A very frustrating afternoon after creating so many chances. Romelu Lukaku came on in the final stages but it did seem Tuchel made his substitutions a little late. Michael Carrick said after the game that he felt disappointed with the draw, he must have been watching a completely different game. We couldn't blame Anthony Taylor for this one and it was definitely two points dropped especially with both Liverpool and Manchester City winning their games. Funniest moment of the match were chants of 'You're just a shit Billy Gilmour,' aimed at Scott McTominay, he also saw the funny side.

DECEMBER 2021

1st December
Premier League
Watford 1-2 Chelsea
Vicarage Road
Attendance: 20,388

Chelsea (3-4-3): Mendy, Chalobah (Ziyech 60), Christensen, Rudiger, Azpilicueta (c) (Lukaku 69), Loftus-Cheek, Saul (Thiago Silva (h-t), Alonso, Mount, Havertz, Pulisic
Chelsea Goals: Mount (29), Ziyech (72)

Watford (4-2-3-1): Bachmann, Femenia, Cathcart, Troost-Ekong, Masina (Rose 12), Louza (Kucka 73), Sissoko, Dennis, Cleverley (Ngakia 85), Joao Pedro, King
Watford Goal: Dennis (43)

Despite Chelsea only having three days to prepare for the game it was certainly an eventful couple of days. Details of dates regarding the Club World Cup were announced with the competition taking place in the United Arab Emirates in early February with two Premier League games away to Brighton and at home to Arsenal affected. Chelsea would join the competition at the semi-final stage.

The Ballon d'Or result was finally announced with five Chelsea players in contention. Azpilicueta came 29th, Mount 19th, Lukaku 12th, Kante 5th and Jorginho 3rd. A great achievement with Lionel Messi taking the prize. Hosted by Didier Drogba it was quite fitting that on the night there was also a prize for the team of the year. That inevitably went to Chelsea!

Things were looking very positive off the pitch until more uncertainty unravelled regarding a new contract for Andreas Christensen which he still hadn't signed. Thomas Tuchel added; "My understanding was that it's a matter of time of a very short period before we have good news. It's on Andreas to act how he acts on the pitch, he needs to act off it and walk the talk because he tells us that he loves Chelsea."

Tuchel had made six changes for the game and it was clear fatigue and injuries was catching up with players. Most notably Saul made his first league start since his debut against Aston Villa and Cesar Azpilicueta replaced the injured Reece James. Looking at the line-up you could be forgiven for thinking it was a Carabao Cup match.

In truth this was probably our worst performance of the season so far and we were very fortunate to come away with all three points, and the players knew it as well. We started the game in a sloppy manner and Watford under Claudio Ranieri were not frightened to have a go. We didn't start the game brightly and play came to a halt after just 12 minutes with the players being taken off the pitch. Players from both teams alerted the referee after a Watford supporter had a cardiac arrest in the stands. The Chelsea medical team assisted the Watford staff in helping the supporter. It was later reported he was taken to hospital in a stable condition with both medical teams receiving a standing ovation.

Play resumed 30 minutes later and it was Chelsea who took the lead through an assured finish from Mason Mount. A well-worked goal with good play from both Marcos Alonso and Kai Havertz. However, it wasn't a surprise when Watford equalised shortly before half-time through Dennis after having the better of the chances. It was the first goal we'd conceded away from home in the Premier League all season. It was clear at the break this was an extremely tough game, Saul was taken off after a very disappointing first-half.

The second-half wasn't much better and Edouard Mendy made some important saves. Our quality did come through with around 20 minutes remaining with Mount now turning provider for substitute Ziyech (who replaced the injured Chalobah) to finish well. We got away with it on the night and Watford probably deserved at least a point. The three points were very welcomed and we remained one point clear at the top. It was also the birth of Edouard Mendy's new song; "Tsamina mina, eh eh Edouard Edouard Mendy, Tsamina mina zangalewa, He comes from Senegal". (The song, 'Waka Waka (This Time For Africa)' by Shakira)

4th December
Premier League
West Ham 3-2 Chelsea
The London Stadium
Attendance: 59,942

Chelsea (3-4-3): Mendy, Christensen, Thiago Silva, Rudiger, James, Jorginho (c), Loftus-Cheek, Alonso (Pulisic 73), Ziyech (Hudson-Odoi 64), Havertz (Lukaku h-t), Mount
Chelsea Goals: Thiago Silva (28), Mount (44)

West Ham United (3-5-2): Fabianski, Dawson, Zouma (Fornals 71), Diop, Coufal, Soucek, Rice, Lanzini (Benrahma 85), Johnson (Masuaku 45), Bowen, Antonio
West Ham United Goals: Lanzini (40 pen), Bowen (56), Masuaku (87)

The day before the match I was back at Stamford Bridge for the Chelsea Annual Lunch. I was fortunate enough to get discounted tickets through the ballot. A great event and an early Christmas present for my dad, where we got meet many ex players and see the likes of Petr Cech, Paulo Ferriera, Thomas Tuchel and Cesar Azpilicueta on stage.

Despite West Ham having a dip in-form I didn't feel that confident going into the game. We needed to play better and the team sheet was encouraging with James and Jorginho coming back into the team. It started well for Chelsea with Thiago Silva heading in Mason Mount's corner. At this point I felt we'd go on to win the game but we gifted West Ham an equaliser after a dreadful back pass from Jorginho. Edouard Mendy in fairness should have cleared it but instead brought down Bowen as he closed him down. West Ham scored from the resulting penalty and it looked like it would be all square going into half-time. Mason Mount had other ideas and scored a truly fantastic volley from Hakim Ziyech's cross.

Bowen was having a great match and equalised on 56 minutes, I would have happily taken a draw at this point. West Ham scored the winner with three minutes to go after Masuaku's poor cross deceived Mendy and went in at the near post. We were unlucky with the winning goal but on the whole it was another disappointing performance. After the weekend's results we dropped down to third in the table. The conclusion of the Champions League group stage was up next.

The football itself came second during this weekend across the country as every club paid tribute to Arthur Labinjo-Hughes on the sixth minute of each game.

8th December
Champions League, Group H, Match Day 6
Zenit St Petersburg 3-3 Chelsea
Gazprom Arena
Attendance: 29,349

Chelsea (3-4-2-1): Kepa, Azpilicueta (c), Christensen, Sarr, Hudson-Odoi (Pulisic 65), James, Barkley (Ziyech 65), Saul (Alonso 75), Mount, Lukaku (Havertz 75), Werner
Chelsea Goals: Werner (2, 85), Lukaku (62)

Zenit St Petersburg (5-4-1): Kritsyuk, Barrios, Lovren, Rakitskyy (Krugovoi 65), Malcom (Erokhin 79), Karavaev, Kuzyaev (Ozdoev 79), Wendel (Mostovoy 51), Santos, Claudinho, Azmoun (Dzyuba 79)
Zenit St Petersburg Goals: Claudinho (38), Azmoun (42), Ozdoev (90)

Leading up to the game there was quite a bit happening off the pitch. Former goal keeper Willy Caballero signed a short deal at Southampton, Tuchel announced that Mateo Kovacic was back fit but then tested positive for Covid-19 and Chelsea drew National League side Chesterfield at home in the F.A Cup third round draw.

Away from the football Prime Minister Boris Johnson continued to deny there had been Christmas parties at Downing Street despite a video obtained by ITV News showing his spokesperson joking about it. Boris later announced that the UK was now on alert level four due to the Omicron variant with people working from home if possible.

Back to the football saw Chelsea travel to Russia to face Zenit St Petersburg in the final group stage match of the Champions League and a first outing for the third kit. After a fantastic win against Juventus we just had to match their result in order to win the group.

It was very clear from the line-up that changes had to be made and this was a difficult time for Chelsea with a heavy fixture schedule and many injuries to key players, although it was intriguing to see Reece James in midfield.

We started the game in the perfect way and took the lead through a tap-in from Timo Werner after a corner from Ross Barkley caused problems. You'd be forgiven for thinking at that point that Chelsea would run out comfortable winners. It wasn't the case and in all honesty the first-half was extremely poor and we deserved to be 2-1 down with Zenit scoring two goals in quick succession shortly before half-time.

The Chelsea equaliser came from Lukaku after some good work from Barkley and Werner. A well-worked Chelsea goal with 30 minutes remaining had us thinking we'd go on and win the match. With just five minutes remaining Timo Werner scored a great goal with a shot on the turn to put us back into the lead. With Juventus winning against Malmo we needed to win to top the group. We couldn't do that and Zenit equalised in injury time with a fantastic finish. A very disappointing result and a real concern considering the amount of goals against us. Despite conceding three, Kepa actually made some crucial saves in the match.

11th December
Premier League
Chelsea 3-2 Leeds United
Stamford Bridge
Attendance: 39,959

Chelsea (3-4-3): Mendy, Azpilicueta (c) (Christensen 74), Thiago Silva, Rudiger, James, Loftus-Cheek, Jorginho, Alonso (Lukaku 87), Mount, Havertz, Werner (Hudson-Odoi 74)
Chelsea Goals: Mount (42), Jorginho (58, 90 pens)

Leeds United (4-3-3): Meslier, Dalla, Ayling, Llorente, Firpo, Shackleton (Klich 59), Roberts, Forshaw, Raphinha (Gelhardt 81), James (Cresswell 88), Harrison
Leeds United Goals: Raphinha (28 pen), Gelhardt 83)

Despite difficult form, as far away as New York, the Empire State Building had been lit up in blue to honour the Champions Of Europe.

Next up, Chelsea v Leeds United. A fixture with so much history especially in the 1970's and 1980's, and one that has been missed in recent years. Don't get me wrong, there's no love lost between the two teams, but it is a league fixture and a rivalry that's needed regularly. It was a fixture during the 20/21 season but during the pandemic there was only a crowd of 2,000 allowed at Stamford Bridge.

As soon as I arrived at Fulham Broadway what was notable more than ever was the police presence on the streets down the Fulham Road. A quick chat at the "cfcuk" stall before heading to the Cock Tavern to see a few of the usual faces. Everyone was buzzing for this one and it had the feel of a very big game despite both teams struggling with injuries. There was also a lot of talk of Leeds fans printing fake A4 email tickets in order to get in the pubs etc. I soon met my dad for a pre-match meal and him reminiscing about the battles with Leeds over the years. Once inside the ground you could feel the atmosphere and as the teams came out it was nice to see the 'OSGOOD 9' banner revealed in the Shed Upper. A nice touch and a reminder of his diving header against Leeds in the 1970 F.A Cup Final replay at Old Trafford. Thomas announced in his pre-match press conference that Jorghino would have to 'play with pain' and he did heroically.

It was a game that had many ups-and-downs with some inconsistent individual performances. Against the run of play Leeds took the lead through a Raphinha penalty after a late challenge from Marcos Alonso. Deservedly Chelsea fought back through Mason Mount and he proceeded to put his finger to his lips in front of the travelling Leeds fans. At half-time I still felt we would win the game but it wouldn't be easy. That was exactly the case despite going 2-1 up with half an hour to go. Jorginho converted his penalty emphatically into the top corner after Rudiger had been fouled. It was a nervy moment as the referee hadn't initially given it and had to look at the monitor after intervention from VAR.

Leeds equalised through substitute Gelhardt with seven minutes remaining after some poor defending. At that point it really felt it was going to be another one of those games where we'd drop points. However, there was enough time for one more big moment in the match. Deep into injury time Rudiger was fouled again in the box and another penalty was awarded. Jorginho again stepped up and this time placed it into the bottom corner. A huge sigh of relief and at the final whistle there was a feeling we had got away with one. It was a much-needed three points with other teams around us also picking up three points. Things boiled over at the final whistle with both sets of players needing to be separated. It was a game full of passion and that was demonstrated at the end, Mason's goal celebration and of course Cesar Azpilicueta giving it back to the Leeds fans when he was substituted and had to walk past them. Much work to be done at this stage but it felt like a big win.

16th December
Premier League
Chelsea 1-1 Everton
Stamford Bridge

Attendance: 39,933

Chelsea (3-4-3): Mendy, Azpilicueta (c) (Chalobah 79), Thiago Silva, Rudiger, James, Loftus-Cheek (Barkley 65), Jorginho, Alonso (Saul 65), Ziyech, Pulisic, Mount
Chelsea Goal: Mount (70)

Everton (4-4-2): Pickford, Kenny, Keane (c), Holgate, Branthwaite, Godfrey, Doucoure, Gomes (Gbamin 70), Iwobi, Simms (Dobbin 62), Gordon (Onyango 90)
Everton Goal: Branthwaite (74)

At the start of the week it was the draw for the Champions League last 16. Chelsea were drawn against Lille, which on paper was the best possible draw avoiding the like of Bayern Munich and Real Madrid. After an error during the draw it was remarkably declared void and would have to take place again that afternoon. A hugely embarrassing moment for UEFA which they blamed on the malfunction of some software. In quite bizarre circumstances we were drawn against Lille again! Even Specsavers on Twitter got in on the act tweeting; 'Announcement; we'll be sponsoring the second #UCLdraw at 2pm'.

On the same day the Premier League announced there were 42 positive cases of Covid-19 from players and staff in the latest round of testing (6th – 12th December). The Premier League had to revert to 'Emergency Measures' and increase the frequency of lateral flow and PCR testing. Tottenham had already had a Europa Conference League game and a league game against Brighton postponed during the weekend and it was same for the midweek Premier League fixture between Brentford and Manchester United. There were real concerns at this stage amongst supporters that football could soon be played behind closed doors again.

The club announced on Tuesday 14th December that a safe standing trial at Stamford Bridge would begin from our fixture against Liverpool on January 2nd. On the Wednesday, Thomas Tuchel announced that both N'Golo Kante and Trevoh Chalobah had returned to full training, Ben Chilwell was still out and Mateo Kovacic was still isolating. Tuchel also stated that 'We want to get back on track defensively' ahead of the Everton match. Edouard Mendy, Jorginho, Romelu Lukaku and N'Golo Kante had all been nominated for the men's FIFA FIFPro World 11 squads.

Thomas Tuchel also spoke about the in-form Conor Gallagher with the club respecting the loan agreement and he would remain at Crystal Palace for the remainder of the season. "We like Gallagher and how well he is doing. Nothing has changed, we see him all the time. There is no regret (about loaning him out)".

Another midweek fixture was postponed, this time Burnley v Watford as Burnley had a number of positive COVID-19 cases in the squad. At this point Brentford had 13 confirmed cases amongst players and first team staff. This had put the Carabao Cup quarter-final against Chelsea into serious doubt.

With the Omicron variant spreading quickly the number of positive cases were increasing rapidly. Sky News reported, "Britons advised not to attend football matches in stadiums and to 'prioritise' events that 'matter to them'. The government were urging the public to be double-jabbed and if they'd already done so to have the booster. A worrying time in general in the build-up to Christmas and in footballing terms the dreaded thought that the game may revert to being played behind closed doors.

The game did go ahead and the team to face Everton was depleted but in all honesty the same issues applied to Everton who were in very poor form under Rafa Benitez. Amongst injuries Chelsea now had four positive cases of COVID-19, Ben Chilwell, Callum Hudson-Odoi, Romelu Lukaku and Timo Werner. Kai Havertz was also out after feeling unwell but his test was negative along with Mateo Kovacic who was still isolating. This meant Christian Pulisic would play through the middle as a 'false 9'. It was an extremely frustrating game with Chelsea once again having many chances but just not converting them. It was Mason Mount however who opened the scoring with 20 minutes remaining. His fourth goal in his last four Premier League matches and a feeling this could've been the match winner. However defensive frailties cost us and Everton against the run of play equalised just four minutes later. A few boos were heard at the final whistle with fans showing their disappointment. The goals we were conceding was alarming and it was a game we most certainly needed to win. A very challenging period for Chelsea in difficult circumstances. Chelsea had a combined 72 shots at home to Everton, Manchester United and Burnley and scored just three goals.

Thomas Tuchel added after the match; "I am not sure why we get punished like this. I see teams concede more chances than we do, we conceded absolutely nothing today and it was a draw".

Chelsea had once again opened the doors of Stamford Bridge for members of the public to have a COVID-19 jab or a booster the day before our trip to Wolves.

19th December
Premier League
Wolverhampton Wanderers 0-0 Chelsea
Molineux
Attendance: 30,631

Chelsea (3-4-3): Mendy, Azpilicueta (c), Thiago Silva, Rudiger, James, Kante, Chalobah (Saul h/t), Alonso, Mount, Pulisic, Ziyech (Kovacic 65)

Wolverhampton Wanderers (3-5-1-1): Sa, Kilman, Coady, Saiss, Hoever, Dendoncker, Neves, Moutinho, Marcal, Podence (Traore 79), Jimenez (Trincao 89)

A very strange weekend of football that saw all of Saturday's matches postponed except for the late kick-off between Leeds and Arsenal.

3,014 Chelsea fans made the trip to Wolverhampton on the Sunday not knowing if the game would go ahead. Chelsea requested that the game should be called off on the morning of the match. The club said there will be players on the bench that are not fit to play but the Premier League rejected this saying we still had 14 players fit to play. Thomas Tuchel said it was a risk for

Kante and Chalobah to come back into the team so quickly. Jorginho and Loftus-Cheek also missed the trip due to injury. The club were said to be "deeply disappointed" by the decision to play the game. The number of Covid-19 cases had risen to seven including players and staff. There were also players that couldn't play due to waiting on results from tests. It seemed unfair it was played, but I was pleased for the travelling Chelsea supporters who didn't make a wasted trip.

The game itself was far from a classic and despite the circumstances surrounding the match it was a decent point. Wolves had the better of the first-half and thought they'd taken an early lead only for the assistant referee to eventually raise his flag. We had a couple of chances as we significantly improved in the second-half. Saul came on at half-time and played well despite his very difficult start to life at Chelsea. Pulisic had a chance for us but it was well saved and there was a shout for a Chelsea penalty on N'Golo Kante in the later stages but it wasn't to be. It was also good to see Mateo Kovacic back on the pitch. A first clean sheet for a while but now in third place and slipping further behind league leaders Manchester City. All eyes were now firmly on what happens next for football in general and whether our quarter-final Carabao Cup tie at Brentford would still go ahead.

22nd December
Carabao Cup Quarter-final
Brentford 0-2 Chelsea
Brentford Community Stadium
Attendance: 16,577

Chelsea (3-4-3): Kepa, Azpilicueta (c), Chalobah, Sarr, Simons (James 66), Kovacic (Jorginho h/t), Saul, Alonso, Barkley (Kante 76), Soonsup-Bell (Pulisic h/t), Vale (Mount 66)
Chelsea Goals: Jansson (o.g 80), Jorginho (pen 85)

Brentford (3-5-2): Fernandez, Sorensen, Jansson (c), Pinnock, Canos, Jensen (Forss 81), Baptiste (Onyeka 74), Janelt (Norgaard 66), Henry (Ghoddos 74), Mbeumo, Wissa (Toney 66)

The day before the match Chelsea legend Gianluca Vialli announced that he was still battling pancreatic cancer stating "The unwanted guest, as I call it, is still here with me. At this moment I am in maintenance mode. The tumour is still there. At times it is more noticeable, at others less so".

There was a win for owner Roman Abramovich off the pitch as he won his defamation claim against Harper Collins, donating the settlement to charity. The game did go ahead with Brentford having many players return but the same couldn't be said for Chelsea. Jorginho's Covid-19 test was a false positive so he was available for selection.

The line-up was to be expected with many changes from Thomas Tuchel. Most notably three debutants from the academy with Harvey Vale, Xavier Simons and Jude Soonsup-Bell all impressing. The only three players that kept their places from the draw at Wolves were Azpilicueta, Kovacic and Saul.

The game was pretty even throughout, however Brentford had the best chances with Kepa making some fine saves and continuing to impress in the competition. Tuchel made use of all five substitutions and they were key in the later stages of the match. Reece James provided a significant assist with just ten minutes remaining with his dangerous cross being turned into his own net by Pontus Jansson. The tie was wrapped up five minutes later when Christian Pulisic was fouled by the Brentford goalkeeper in the penalty area. Jorginho stepped up and finished with ease sending The Blues through. On reflection it was a very positive result in very difficult circumstances. The Chelsea fans were superb throughout despite the small allocation. A new song was heard to the tune of the Willian song;

"Kovacic our Croatian man,
He left Madrid and he left Milan,
He signed for Frank and said fuck Zidane,
He signed for Chelsea on a transfer ban."

The draw for the semi-final was made shortly after the match with Chelsea facing Tottenham over two legs with the first-leg at

Stamford Bridge. The other semi-final would see Arsenal play Liverpool.

26th December
Premier League
Aston Villa 1-3 Chelsea
Villa Park
Attendance: 41,907

Chelsea (3-4-3): Mendy, Chalobah (Lukaku h/t), Thiago Silva (Christensen 52), Rudiger, James, Kante (Kovacic 63), Jorginho (c), Alonso, Mount, Pulisic, Hudson-Odoi
Chelsea Goals: Jorginho (pen 34, 90), Lukaku (56)

Aston Villa (4-3-3): Martinez, Cash, Konsa, Mings (c), Targett, Sanson (El Ghazi 76), Douglas Luiz, J Ramsey, Buendia (Chukwuemeka 73), Ings (Traore 73), Watkins
Aston Villa Goal: James (o.g 28)

The number of games was relentless for Chelsea with many other clubs having games postponed. Aston Villa away is never an easy fixture, especially the evening Sky Sports game on Boxing Day when most are expecting an upset. It was just two wins in our previous six league games and Manchester City had already beaten Leicester earlier in the day. Aston Villa manager Steven Gerrard missed the game due to testing positive for Covid-19.

We started the game well and despite hitting the bar it was Villa who took the lead on 28 minutes as Reece James stretched to block Matt Target's cross and the ball skimmed off his head which went through Mendy's hands. We deservedly got back in the game shortly after as Jorginho converted from the spot after Hudson-Odoi was fouled.

Romelu Lukaku came on at half-time and made a huge impact scoring a great header from a pinpoint cross from Hudson-Odoi. We were very much in control at this stage and had other chances to wrap the game up earlier. It was injury time when the points were secured. A great run from Lukaku using his pace and power eventually saw him being brought down in the box. Jorginho stepped up again and scored again. It was now six penalties scored in his last six games. A very good result and team performance but Hudson-Odoi and Lukaku really made the difference. The only downside was Thiago Silva going off injured, however this was not as serious as first thought.

29th December
Premier League
Chelsea 1-1 Brighton & Hove Albion
Stamford Bridge
Attendance: 40,088

Chelsea (3-4-3): Mendy, Azpilicueta (c), Christensen (Chalobah h/t), Rudiger, James (Alonso 27), Jorginho, Kovacic, Pulisic, Mount, Lukaku, Hudson-Odoi (Kante 67)
Chelsea Goal: Lukaku (28)

Brighton & Hove Albion (4-3-3): Sanchez, Veltman, Burn, Cucarella, Lamptey (Mwepu 66), Lallana (c), Bissouma, March, Moder (Alzate 88), Maupay, MacAllister (Welbeck 80)
Brighton & Hove Albion Goal: Welbeck (90)

On the 28th December I tested positive for Covid-19 as did other members of my household which meant missing the next three games at Stamford Bridge. The day before the Brighton game there was some great news that John Terry was returning to Stamford Bridge in an Academy coaching consultancy role. John added on his Instagram page; "I'm delighted to announce that I'm coming home, and have taken up a consultancy role at the Chelsea FC academy. As well as delivering on-field coaching sessions I will be involved in coaching discussions and mentoring our academy players."

Leading up to the match it seemed quite a few people were falling ill as many spare tickets were becoming available on social media platforms. In all honesty I'm pleased I wasn't at this one as it was poor viewing at times with much frustration in the crowd. It was probably one of our poorest performances of the season and under Thomas Tuchel.

Romelu Lukaku made his first league start since October 16th and it was the Belgian who headed Chelsea into the lead against the run of play. More injury problems were coming our way, this time it was Reece James who was forced off after playing left-wing-back to combat former blue Tariq Lamptey. Andreas Christensen was also replaced in the first-half due to injury. The team was very disjointed and Pulisic moved to right wing-back, with Alonso now on the other side.

Brighton were well organised but hadn't come to defend, they were dominating the game in all areas. Although on another day we might have got a penalty when Hudson-Odoi's cross was handled and Mason had a goal disallowed for a foul. However the overall performance was very disappointing. Just when it felt we had got away with a very fortunate three points Brighton equalised in injury time through substitute Danny Welbeck. A real blow to any chance of a title challenge we thought we might still have. Brighton came away with a decent point but on another night it may have been all three. It was Brighton's first ever league goal at Stamford Bridge. Our home form was quite alarming with The Blues dropping 11 points from leading positions in the Premier League during this season which was now more than the whole of the 2020/21 season.

Thomas Tuchel was clearly still very frustrated after the match and stated; "We have seven COVID-19 cases and four or five out with injuries. How should we compete in a title race? It would be stupid. Everybody else has a full squad and everybody available. I simply don't know what (more) I can expect from my players."

JANUARY 2022

2nd January
Premier League
Chelsea 2-2 Liverpool
Stamford Bridge
Attendance: 40,072

Chelsea (3-4-3): Mendy, Chalobah (Jorginho 70), Thiago Silva, Rudiger, Azpilicueta (c), Kante, Kovacic, Alonso, Mount, Havertz (Hudson-Odoi 79), Pulisic
Chelsea Goals: Kovacic (43), Pulisic (45)

Liverpool (4-3-3): Kelleher, Alexander-Arnold, Konate, Van Dijk, Tsimikas, Milner (Keita 69), Henderson (c), Fabinho, Salah, Jota (Oxlade-Chamberlin 69), Mane (Jones 90)
Liverpool Goals: Mane (9), Salah (26)

Thomas Tuchel spoke prior to the game with news that Ben Chilwell would now need surgery and would miss the remainder of the season and what the situation was regarding recalling Emerson Palmieri from his loan. "We are looking into it because we now have a new situation with Ben Chilwell so of course we look into whether we can do something and what we can do. One of the possibilities and the players we know and that we love as a person is Emerson but we need to check. We are not into details. We are discussing and reflecting and this will go on for the coming days, maybe weeks".

There was also a lot of transfer talk around Everton left back Lucas Digne joing Chelsea permanently or on loan.

After more than a decade of service to the club as a player, coach and ambassador, Tore Andre Flo left Chelsea to take over at Sogndal in his native country Norway. New Years Eve also saw former coach Steve Holland (MBE) and Chelsea women's manager Emma Hayes (OBE) receive honours from the Queen.

However, the biggest news broke on the morning of New Year's Eve that shocked world football. An interview from Romelu Lukaku for Sky Sports Italy that had been filmed three weeks prior to its release. It was the last thing Thomas Tuchel needed on the eve of such a big match.

Romelu Lukaku; "Now it's the right time to share my feelings. I have always said that I have Inter in my heart. I know I will return to Inter, I really hope so. I am in love with Italy, this is the right moment to talk and let people know what really happened.

Physically I am fine. But I'm not happy with the situation at Chelsea. Tuchel has chosen to play with another system. I won't give up, I'll be professional. I am not happy with the situation but I am professional and I can't give up now.

If there had been the offer of a new contract from Inter last summer as I wanted.... we would not be doing this interview now here from London, but quietly from Milano."

It really was a bombshell hearing these quotes from Lukaku and then watching the interview itself. Understandably this went down terribly with the supporters, Thomas Tuchel and the club itself.

Thomas Tuchel responded; "Nobody in this building was aware he is unhappy so that is why it is a surprise. We need to check, wait and see what Romelu says and deal with it.

We don't like it, it brings noise we don't need. We don't want to make more of it than what it is. It's easy to take lines out of context and make headlines. I don't like it it's noise we don't need it doesn't help."

The news broke on the morning of the Liverpool game that Tuchel would leave Lukaku out of the squad. A big call but the right one in my opinion. It also sent a message to the other players and any other future signings that no one player is bigger than the club. The club were said to be fuming with Lukaku's comments having invested near to £100m for him in the summer and considered one of the most high profile players.

The game itself was an absolute cracker and for the neutral I would imagine it was a very entertaining watch. There was no Jurgen Klopp in the dugout for Liverpool as he tested positive for Covid-19 prior to the match. Thiago Silva returned to the back three after coming off injured against Brighton, Kai Havertz replaced Lukaku up top and Kante and Kovacic took the central midfield roles.

The game started with instant controversy when Sadio Mane clattered into Cesar Azpilicueta with his elbow after just six seconds. Referee Anthony Taylor gave a yellow card which really should've been a red. We started the game well but found ourselves 1-0 down as Mane capitalised on an individual error from Trevoh Chalobah. It wasn't long until Liverpool made it two after some great individual skill from former blue Mohammed Salah. Stamford Bridge was in shock as we were playing some good football but there was always a worry Liverpool could run away with it.

However two goals in four minutes before half-time completely changed the game. Mateo Kovacic pulled one back from a Marcos Alonso corner. The ball was punched clear by Kelleher, jogging backwards Kovacic had to adjust his feet before volleying the ball that evaded the stretching goal keeper and went in off the post. Undoubtedly an early contender for goal of the season.

Stamford Bridge was back in full voice and we were back on level terms as we approached half-time. A clever flick from Kante allowed Pulisic to go through on goal, and he calmly hit the ball on the half-volley into the roof of the net. The noise was deafening and no more than we deserved.

Edouard Mendy was heading off to the African Cup Of Nations straight after the match but he didn't leave without making some fantastic saves in the second-half. Chelsea had some chances to win it as well but on reflection it felt like a very good point especially in the circumstances leading up to the match. Kovacic, Kante, Pulisic and Mendy were the stand-out players in a very good and spirited team performance.

5th January
Carabao Cup Semi-final, First-Leg
Chelsea 2-0 Tottenham Hotspur
Stamford Bridge
Attendance: 37,868

Chelsea (3-4-1-2): Kepa, Azpilicueta (c), (Vale 89), Rudiger, Sarr, Ziyech (Pulisic 79), Jorginho, Saul (Loftus-Cheek 73), Alonso, Mount (Kovacic 73), Lukaku, Havertz (Werner h/t)
Chelsea Goals: Havertz (5), Davies (o.g 34)

Tottenham Hotspur (3-4-3): Lloris (c), Tanganga, Sanchez, Davies, Emerson Royal, Skipp (Winks 73), Hojbjerg, Doherty (Ndombele h/t), Moura (Gil 79), Kane, Son (Lo Celso 79)

With all the noise around the club being quite negative regarding the Lukaku situation it was nice to hear some positive news. Thiago Silva signed a new one-year contract extension for the following season. He's been exceptional since he arrived, I don't think many would have predicted he'd spend at least three years at the club.

All eyes were now firmly on the Carabao Cup and Tottenham manager Antonio Conte returning to Stamford Bridge for the first time since leaving Chelsea. Thiago Silva and N'Golo Kante missed the match after testing positive for Covid-19 with Thomas Tuchel confirming both were due to play. Another battle Chelsea had to face whilst Liverpool had their semi-final with Arsenal postponed despite it later being confirmed suspiciously that they had many 'false positives' in the squad.

Despite our difficulties off the pitch it was advantage Chelsea going into the second-leg. We dominated the game from start to finish and if anything it was a little frustrating we couldn't completely kill the tie going into the second-leg. It also has to be said how poor Tottenham were and despite their fans having the whole 'Shed End' their support coincided with their performance. Kai Havertz settled the nerves very early on with an assured finish after being fed through by Marcos Alonso, despite Kai breaking his finger in the process. Chelsea dominance continued and it was 2-0 shortly before half-time after a comedy error from the Tottenham defence with the ball coming off Davies last.

Our dominance continued but couldn't manage to get another goal with Tottenham rarely threatening Kepa's goal. The best players on the night were Saul, Ziyech, Sarr and Alonso. It was good to see Lukaku back in the team who worked hard and also seeing academy prospect Harvey Vale come on towards the end of the game for his home debut. There was also a milestone for Ruben Loftus-Cheek who had now made 100 appearances for Chelsea. The Chelsea fans continued to sing "Tottenham get battered everywhere they go" towards the end of the game but it was only half-time with a second-leg to come.

8th January
F.A Cup 3rd Round
Chelsea 5-1 Chesterfield
Stamford Bridge
Attendance: 39,795

Chelsea (3-5-2): Bettinelli, Christensen (Baker 59), Sarr, Hall, Ziyech, Pulisic (Vale 58), Saul, Kovacic (c) (Loftus-Cheek h/t), Hudson-Odoi (Barkley 66), Lukaku (Havertz h/t), Werner
Chelsea Goals: Werner (6), Hudson-Odoi (18), Lukaku (20), Christensen (39), Ziyech (55 pen)

Chesterfield (4-3-2-1): Loach, Kerr, Gunning (c) (Grimes 60), Croll, Whittle, King (Miller h/t), Oyeleke (Maguire 73), Weston, Kellermann (Asante 66), Khan (Mandeville h/t), Tshimanga
Chesterfield Goal: Asante (80)

Attention turned to the F.A Cup 3rd round with National League leaders Chesterfield visiting Stamford Bridge. It was announced by the F.A that there would be no replays in the third and fourth round ties and all clubs must participate despite Covid-19 related issues. Chesterfield took the whole 'Shed End' and were in full voice throughout. Again Covid-19 stopped me from attending this one and it was now four home matches in a row that I missed. I was particularly gutted as I was planning on going with my dad and brothers.

The famous competition was now in it's 150th year and it was 25 years since our special victorious F.A Cup campaign in 1997. A Wembley final against Middlesbrough which could have quite easily been Chesterfield. It was also a nice touch that Chelsea's 1970 F.A Cup-winning hero David Webb had a special connection with the game as his son Danny Webb was in the Chesterfield dug out as the club's assistant manager.

Despite inevitable changes to the line-up Chelsea were in cruise control from the very start. A tap-in for Timo Werner got the ball rolling before Callum Hudson-Odoi curled a beauty into the corner from outside the box. Just two minutes later it was 3-0 and an important one for Romelu Lukaku to let his football do the talking. An easy finish assisted by 17 year old debutant Lewis Hall who was outstanding throughout the game and was deservedly awarded Man Of The Match. Five minutes before half-time Andreas Christensen made it 4-0 with a looping header. At the break you really thought Chelsea could go on and score many more.

Credit to Chesterfield they kept going and so did their travelling supporters. Hakim Ziyech made it 5-0 from the penalty spot after Christian Pulisic was fouled in the penalty area. Substitutions were inevitably made and the game did start to fizzle out. However, there was one last big moment in the match and it went to Chesterfield. As Bettinelli spilled an initial shot Asante was on hand to tap-in the rebound from close-range. The 'Shed End' erupted behind the goal which was a wonderful moment for the Chesterfield fans and highlighted the magic of the F.A Cup with a non league side scoring at the Champions of Europe.

The game finished 5-1 and Chelsea were drawn at home to League One side Plymouth Argyle in the fourth round, the two teams last playing a competitive match against each other in 1989. It was a great weekend of F.A Cup action with some significant upsets. Cambridge winning at Newcastle and Nottingham Forest beating Arsenal being the highlights.

12th January
Carabao Cup Semi-final, Second-Leg
Tottenham Hotspur 0-1 Chelsea
Tottenham Hotspur Stadium
Attendance: 45,603

Chelsea (4-4-2): Kepa, Azpilicueta (c), Christensen (Thiago Silva 66), Rudiger, Sarr, Mount (Ziyech 66), Jorginho (Loftus-Cheek 82), Kovacic (Kante 77), Hudson-Odoi, Lukaku, Werner (Alonso 66)
Chelsea Goal: Rudiger (18)

Tottenham Hotspur (3-4-3): Gollini, Tanganga, Sanchez, Davies, Emerson Royal, Winks (Skipp 81), Hojbjerg, Doherty (Sessegnon 65), Lo Celso (Gil 71), Kane (c), Moura

Leading up to the match the CPS confirmed that the 'rent boy' chant directed towards Chelsea players and supporters is a hate crime and not 'harmless banter' as some have tried to claim.

Billy Gilmour returned to Stamford Bridge with rehabilitation on an injured ankle suffered whilst on loan at Norwich City.

This was a huge game and inevitably Chelsea sold out the 5,792 allocation instantly and could have sold a lot more, especially with empty seats noticeable in home stands. Just like the first-leg Chelsea completely dominated the game and never looked uncomfortable having already won the first-leg 2-0. Shortly before the 20 minute mark came the opening goal. A corner from Mason Mount saw the goalkeeper come rushing out only for Antonio Rudiger to beat him to it with his brave header coming off the cross bar and into the net. If you didn't watch the match and just read about it you could be fooled into believing Tottenham were unlucky on the night. This was not the case. They had two penalties overturned by VAR but rightly so. Rudiger's foul was clearly outside the box and Kepa won the ball cleanly against Lucas Moura. Harry Kane also thought he'd equalised but was rightly deemed as being offside. Kepa had made some decent saves throughout the game but we always looked in control.

No doubt Chelsea could have gone up a gear but we really didn't need to. Both legs were very comfortable and we didn't even concede a goal. A great night that saw Chelsea back at Wembley and we'd have to wait another week to know if it would be Liverpool or Arsenal in the final.

15th January
Premier League
Manchester City 1-0 Chelsea
Etihad Stadium
Attendance: 53,319

Chelsea (3-4-2-1): Kepa, Azpilicueta (c), Thiago Silva, Rudiger, Sarr, Alonso (Mount 81), Kante, Kovacic, Ziyech (Hudson-Odoi 69), Pulisic (Werner 69), Lukaku

Manchester City (4-2-3-1): Ederson, Walker, Stones, Laporte, Cancelo, Rodrigo, De Bruyne (c) (Gundogan 84), Bernado, Sterling, Grealish, Foden (Jesus 88)
Manchester City Goal: De Bruyne (70)

The lead up to Manchester City away saw Kenedy return to Stamford Bridge after a loan spell at Flamengo. A decision made by Chelsea as injuries, Covid-19 and a very busy schedule impacted the team. Lewis Baker however joined Stoke City in a permanent deal.

With the game being a 12:30pm kick-off on the Saturday it was a very early start for the travelling Chelsea supporters with many of them taking Champions League shaped balloons with them into the away end. The fans were up for it but the team were not. Unfortunately Andreas Christensen tested positive for Covid-19 with Thiago Silva replacing him. Jorginho was rested so Kovacic came in to partner Kante.

In all fairness it was a lacklustre Chelsea performance and a game we didn't deserve anything from. Lukaku had a great chance to shoot but played in an offside Ziyech and also had the option of Alonso to his left. Lukaku had another chance but

Ederson saved comfortably. Although at half-time it appeared we were doing well I felt it was only a matter of time before City scored especially with Kepa keeping us in the game with some fine saves. The goal itself came from Kevin De Bruyne with just 20 minutes remaining but it was coming! A shot from outside the box, unfortunately for Kepa he took a slight step to the right before the ball was aiming for his left. He couldn't reach it and even at 1-0 I felt there was no way back.

There is no shame in losing to Manchester City but it was the overall performance that disappointed so many. The likes of Ziyech, Pulisic and Lukaku came under the most criticism with the main positive being Malang Sarr in defence. Many fans including myself were also very surprised Mason Mount didn't start the game. The North London derby was postponed as requested from Arsenal which caused much controversy as they only had one case of Covid-19. They had injuries like most teams and it was felt they should have played it using players from the development squad and not loaning out first team players that they had. It was now the 21st Premier League game to be postponed with only Chelsea and Manchester City not having one.

18th January
Premier League
Brighton & Hove Albion 1-1 Chelsea
Amex Stadium
Attendance: 30,880

Chelsea (4-2-2-2): Kepa, Azpilicueta (c), Thiago Silva, Rudiger, Alonso, Kante, Jorginho (Kovacic 80), Ziyech, Mount, Lukaku (Havertz 80), Hudson-Odoi (Werner 80)
Chelsea Goal: Ziyech (28)

Brighton & Hove Albion (4-1-4-1): Sanchez, Veltman, Webster (c), Burn, Cucurella, Alzate, Lamptey (March 76), Gross (Maupay 62), MacAllister, Welbeck (Trossard 62), Moder
Brighton & Hove Albion Goal: Webster (60)

A rearranged midweek game away at Brighton was not ideal with the fixture schedule absolutely relentless. In the few days leading up to the game former Chelsea manager Rafa Benitez was sacked by Everton after losing to relegation threatened Norwich City and Frank Lampard was tipped as a possible replacement. Thomas Tuchel, Edouard Mendy and Emma Hayes all won awards at FIFA's 'The Best' ceremony.

It has to be said this was another tired and lethargic performance by Chelsea. Even with Jorginho, Mount and Hudson-Odoi back in the starting 11 we didn't deserve to take all three points. Our goal was a positive which came out of nothing after a 25 yard strike from Hakim Ziyech found the bottom corner. It was a strange reaction when it went in with the players celebrating in a very low key manner. Even at that stage we didn't kick on and really fight for what would have been a three valuable points.

Brighton equalised with half an hour to go from Webster's header. Most Chelsea fans could see it coming and on reflection Brighton may feel disappointed they didn't win it. Thomas Tuchel left all his substitutions until ten minutes from time and although we rallied it was too late by then. There was an air of concern at this point with only one win in the last seven league games. We remained in third position but teams below could certainly catch up with their games in hand.

23rd January
Premier League
Chelsea 2-0 Tottenham Hotpsur
Stamford Bridge
Attendance: 40,020

Chelsea (4-1-4-1): Kepa, Azpilicueta (c), Thiago Silva, Rudiger, Sarr, Jorginho (Kante 73), Ziyech (Saul 90), Mount, Kovacic, Hudson-Odoi (Alonso 87), Lukaku
Chelsea Goals: Ziyech (47), Thiago Silva (55)

Tottenham Hotspur (4-4-2): Lloris (c), Tanganga (Skipp 56), Dier, Sanchez, Davies, Doherty, Winks (Gil 88), Hojberg,

Sessegnon (Luca Moura 56), Kane, Bergwijn

My first game back after Covid-19 and despite already beating Tottenham three times this season it was another huge game. I was nervous and no way did I feel Tottenham would be as poor as they were in the Carabao Cup games. Despite the disappointing draw at Brighton in the week there was some good news with both Jorginho and Kante being named in the FIFA Pro Team of the year. It would also be a repeat of the 2005 League Cup Final with Chelsea facing Liverpool as they eased past Arsenal at the Emirates.

It was reported that the players had a meeting to discuss indifferent performances, led by captain Cesar Azpilicueta. Me and my dad were up for this one as was the whole of Stamford Bridge with a great atmosphere.

In literally the first minute of the game we really should have taken the lead through Lukaku who couldn't keep his shot on the half volley down after some great play from Mason Mount. We had some other great chances to take the lead before half-time but just couldn't find a breakthrough. I felt a bit frustrated at the break and wondered if it would be another game where we dominated but couldn't take maximum points.

However, just two minutes after the re-start those frustrations went away and we deservedly took the lead through a wonderful strike from Hakim Ziyech on his left foot from outside the box. He was having a very good game and was unlucky not to make it 2-0 soon after. It wasn't long until we had a two goal cushion as Thiago Silva headed in Mason Mount's free kick.

Tottenham were barely in the game and the away end was emptying very fast in the closing minutes. It could have been more but on reflection it was a very good performance and result and now four victories against them without conceding a single goal. Gianfranco Zola spoke of Ziyech's goal stating, 'He had a very quick mind to see the shot and place it. So it's tremendous quality from him. Unbelievable! He is one of those guys that you pay to go and watch.

A two week winter break followed before our next match but there was certainly no shortage of news. Claudio Ranieri was sacked as Watford manager after a poor run of results and Frank Lampard was appointed the new manager of Everton with Joe Edwards and Ashley Cole joining his backroom team. We also saw the close of the January transfer window which saw very little activity at Stamford Bridge to the frustration of many supporters.

Kenedy was added to the winter Premier League squad and given the number 23 shirt. Mateo Kovacic won the Premier League Goal Of The Month for his strike against Liverpool.

Heading into the shortest month of the year it was one where Chelsea would compete in no less than five competitions.

FEBRUARY 2022

5th February
F.A Cup 4th Round
Chelsea 2-1 Plymouth Argyle (AET)
Stamford Bridge
Attendance: 39,959

Chelsea (4-2-3-1): Kepa, Azpilicueta (c) (Chalobah 112), Christensen (Alonso h/t), Rudiger, Sarr, Joringho, Kovacic, Ziyech, Mount (Saul 97), Hudson-Odoi (Havertz 64), Lukaku
Chelsea Goals: Azpilicueta (41), Alonso (105)

Plymouth Argyle (3-5-2): Cooper, Edwards (c), Wilson, Scarr, Gillesphey, Grant (Law 95), Camara (Broom 94), Houghton, Mayor (Randall 77), Garrick (Hardie 68), Jephcott (Ennis 58)
Plymouth Argyle Goal: Gillesphey (8)

Attentions turned back to the F.A Cup with Plymouth Argyle the visitors to Stamford Bridge who were fighting for promotion from League One. Far from a classic match and one many fans will probably forget. Not for me, a special personal moment as I took my eight-year-old son Jack to his very first game. Before the match the news broke that Thomas Tuchel had tested positive for Covid-19 and the team would be lead by his assistants Arno Michels and Zsolt Lowe.

An early Saturday 12:30pm kick-off was perfect and it was apparent inside the ground that many kids were attending with the hope of a bag full of goals. Even with a full strength Chelsea team it wasn't the case and after just eight minutes the unthinkable happened with Plymouth taking the lead through a clever header from a free kick. Chelsea really started to dominate play and we managed to hit the woodwork three times in the first-half. Our equaliser finally came shortly before the break through captain Cesar Azpilicueta with a clever flick. A wonderful goal after which I lifted Jack high into the air. A fantastic personal moment and a first goal of the season for Cesar.

By the end of the 90 minutes, we'd had 35 shots and 20 corners, with the Plymouth goalkeeper Cooper making some great saves. There was however always a feeling that Plymouth could score also. Going into extra-time the nerves were certainly there as I was just desperate for Jack to see Chelsea win in his first game. Marcos Alonso finally got the goal at the end of the first period of extra-time after some good work from Timo Werner and Kai Havertz. A huge sigh of relief but another great moment. The drama was not over with Plymouth being awarded a penalty with three minutes left to play after a foul from Malang Sarr. A really nervy moment but Kepa Arrizabalaga saved as he had done a number of times throughout the season. A far from convincing display but Jack loved every minute and asked when we could go to another match.

9th February
Club World Cup Semi-final
Al Hilal 0-1 Chelsea
Mohammed Bin Zayed Stadium, Abu Dhabi
Attendance: 19,175

Chelsea (3-4-3): Kepa, Christensen, Thiago Silva, Rudiger, Azpilicueta (c), Jorginho (Kante h/t), Kovacic, Alonso (Sarr 87), Ziyech (Mount 72), Lukaku, Havertz
Chelsea Goal: Lukaku (32)

Al Hilal (4-2-3-1): Almuaiouf, Alburayk, Jang, Al Bulayhi, Alshahrani, Kanno, Cuellar, Marega, Pereira (Carrillo 82), Aldawsari (Michael 82), Ighalo

There was no time to rest after Plymouth took Chelsea to extra-time in the F.A Cup as the team flew straight out to Abu Dhabi to prepare for the Club World Cup. The next day we found out that we would play Luton Town away in the fifth round of the F.A Cup.

In the evening all eyes were on the AFCON Final and Edouard Mendy was victorious with Senegal after beating Egypt in a penalty shootout. Another fantastic achievement for Edouard who would later join up with the Chelsea squad after a victory parade. After a couple of days preparation Chelsea would face Al Hilal from Saudi Arabia in the Club World Cup. It was great to see the social media posts leading up to the match with many Chelsea fans making the trip to Abu Dhabi, but for fans back home it was a strange one watching it live on E4.

Many tipped Chelsea to cruise the game but it was far from easy. A competition that wasn't getting a great deal of media coverage but a trophy that still eluded Chelsea. We had the better of the match with possession and chances but did struggle at times. The out-of-form Romelu Lukaku scored the all important goal from close-range after some good work on the left from Kai Havertz. It could have been 2-0 before the break but Kai could only hit the post from a tight angle.

The second-half was lacklustre in all honesty and Kepa made two fantastic saves to ensure we progressed to the Final where we'd play Brazilian side Palmeiras. Mateo Kovacic was named Man Of The Match but there were also good performances from Ziyech and of course Kepa.

12th February
Club World Cup Final
Chelsea 2-1 Palmeiras (AET)
Mohammed Bin Zayed Stadium, Abu Dhabi
Attendance: 32,871

Chelsea (3-4-2-1): Mendy, Christensen (Sarr f/t), Thiago Silva, Rudiger, Azpilicueta (c), Kante, Kovacic (Ziyech f/t), Hudson-Odoi (Saul 76), Mount (Pulisic 31), Lukaku (Werner 76), Havertz
Chelsea Goals: Lukaku (55), Havertz (Pen, 117)

Palmeiras (4-2-3-1): Weverton, Rocha, Gomez (c), Luan, Piquerez, Danilo, Ze Rafael (Jailson 60), Dudu (Rafael Navarro 103), Veiga (Atuesta 76), Scarpa, Rony (Wesley 76)
Palmeiras Goal: Veiga (Pen 64)

Chelsea had a huge boost the night before the game with Thomas Tuchel arriving in Abu Dhabi after recovering from Covid-19. The togetherness of the squad and his backroom team was apparent as he greeted everyone. For me it wasn't necessarily the competition itself it was the fact it was the one trophy Chelsea hadn't won. Most notable to the line-up was Edouard Mendy back in goal. The in-form Hakim Ziyech was named as a substitute.

It has to be said the game itself wasn't great and at times felt like one of those Asia Trophy pre-season tournaments. Palmeiras were well supported in the stadium and making plenty of noise in a competition that means so much to them. They were a very organised team and were more than capable of causing us problems. It quickly felt that this was going to be far from easy for Chelsea. We suffered a huge blow after half an hour with Mason Mount going off injured. Goalless at half-time was an accurate reflection of the game.

Just ten minutes into the second-half came the breakthrough. A wonderful pinpoint cross on the left-hand side from Hudson-Odoi saw Romelu Lukaku use his strength and power to head in emphatically. A really good goal and despite his difficulties at Chelsea Lukaku had now scored big goals in both games. We didn't really kick on after that and it cost us when Palmeiras equalised from the penalty spot after Thiago Silva had handled.

The game went to extra-time and I had a feeling it would go all the way to penalties as neither side looked clinical. With just three minutes left on the clock Chelsea were awarded a penalty. As the Palmeiras players tried to delay the taking of the penalty it appeared Cesar Azpilicueta was taking it as he was holding onto the ball standing by the spot. As the commotion calmed Cesar handed the ball to Kai Havertz. It was all a tactic so that Kai could focus away from all the drama. Havertz stepped up and expertly sent the goal keeper the wrong way. Ecstatic scenes followed by the players and supporters with Kai taking his shirt off. Another wonderful moment for him and Chelsea, Palmeiras later had a player sent off and it was then that you knew Chelsea were going to see out a very difficult game and be crowned 'CHAMPIONS OF THE WORLD'.

I was so relieved and felt like I'd kicked every ball. Chelsea had now won every trophy available. A wonderful achievement and with captain Cesar Azpilicueta the first Chelsea player to do it. Thiago Silva was named player of the tournament who was again class throughout. The celebrations were there for everyone to see with owner Roman Abramovich in the heart of it all.

19th February
Premier League
Crystal Palace 0-1 Chelsea
Selhurst Park
Attendance: 25,109

Chelsea (4-1-4-1): Mendy, Christensen, Thiago Silva, Rudiger, Sarr (Alonso 74), Jorginho (c) (Loftus-Cheek 74), Ziyech, Kante (Kovacic 74), Pulisic, Havertz, Lukaku
Chelsea Goals: Ziyech (89)

Crystal Palace (4-3-3): Guaita, Clyne, Guehi, Anderson, Mitchell. McArthur (c) (Mateta 90), Kouyate, Schlupp, Olise, Ayew (Eze 85), Zaha

Chelsea were back in Premier League action for the first time in a month with a trip to Selhurst Park. Storm Eunice had hit the UK in the days before which caused a lot of disruption to travel. However, the fans that did make it to the game saw Chelsea wearing the yellow away kit with a certain gold badge in the centre of it. Cesar Azpilicueta, Callum Hudson-Odoi and Mason Mount all missed out through injury. Reece James was edging closer and closer to a comeback.

We made really hard work of this game and were fortunate to come away with three points. We had some half chances but

Palace also had chances they really should have done better with. We thought the breakthrough had come with 15 minutes to go only for VAR to confirm Ziyech was offside despite him finishing well. Just as it seemed it would finish goalless Marcos Alonso sent in a great cross from the left-hand side and Ziyech finished well on his left foot at the far post. Zaha had a good chance to equalise but Chelsea held on. A lacklustre performance but a very good three points. Chelsea fans serenaded the players at the final whistle with "NANANANANANANANA, CHAMPIONS OF THE WORLD, OF THE WORLD, CHAMPIONS OF THE WORLD...."

Much talk after the game was about Romelu Lukaku with many moans and groans. A mixture of lack of service to him but Rom himself not actively involving himself in the game. He had just seven touches in the whole match. Just two in the first-half and one of those was from kick-off. Opta Stats confirmed it was the fewest in a single game for a player with 90+ minutes played since the data was made available in 2003/04.

Manchester City were now just six points clear of second placed Liverpool after dramatically losing at home to Tottenham. Chelsea were in third place, 13 points off the top.

22nd February
Champions League, Last 16, First-Leg
Chelsea 2-0 Lille
Stamford Bridge
Attendance: 38,832

Chelsea (3-4-3): Mendy, Christensen, Thiago Silva, Rudiger, Azpilicueta (c), Kante, Kovacic (Loftus-Cheek 51), Alonso (Sarr 80), Ziyech (Saul 60), Havertz, Pulisic (Werner 80)
Chelsea Goals: Havertz (8), Pulisic (63)

Lille (4-4-1-1): Jardim, Celik, J Fonte (c), S Botman, Djalo (Gudmundsson 76), Sanches (Ben Arfa 81), Xeka, Andre, Bamba, Onana (Yilmaz 65), David (Zhegrova 81)

Chelsea were back in action just three days after the Crystal

Palace game and it was the return of the Champions League as we faced French side Lille at Stamford Bridge in the last 16, first-leg. Despite a quick turnaround there was much talk in the press of Eden Hazard returning to Chelsea on loan for the next season. Prime Minister Boris Johnson had announced all Covid-19 regulations were now coming to an end and on a separate matter also stated that it was inconceivable that the Champions League Final should take place in St Petersburg in Russia given the political situation in Ukraine. Many also still had plenty to say about Romelu Lukaku who Thomas Tuchel decided to leave out of the first 11.

A full house at Stamford Bridge welcomed the newly crowned Champions Of The World and saw Reece James, Ben Chilwell and Callum Hudson-Odoi parade the trophy around the pitch pre-match. Ben Chilwell seemed much stronger on his feet and didn't seem to have many issues in his movement when the water sprinkler came on!

The performance was very positive and the best we'd played in weeks. Kai Havertz was up top and opened the scoring from a good header after just eight minutes and had two good chances prior to that, the man for the big occasion. There was a fitting tribute on 31 minutes with supporters on their feet applauding Jamal Edwards who sadly lost his life. A British music entrepreneur, DJ, founder of the online music platform SB.TV and a huge Chelsea fan.

We finally got our second goal midway through the second-half. A fantastic run from N'Golo Kante and finished superbly by Christian Pulisic. A very solid result going into the second-leg. The only disappointment was Mateo Kovacic and Hakim Ziyech were forced off through injury. Kante, Pulisic and Thiago Silva were the stand-out performers on a very positive evening. Despite a few moans and groans about performances leading up to this match Chelsea had now only had two defeats in the last 32 games. Chelsea also became the first English team in history of the European Cup / Champions League to win five consecutive home matches without conceding a goal. All eyes were now firmly on Wembley.

27th February
Carabao Cup Final
Chelsea 0-0 Liverpool (Liverpool won 11-10 on penalties)
Wembley Stadium
Attendance: 85,512

Chelsea (3-4-3): Mendy (Kepa 120), Chalobah, Thiago Silva, Rudiger, Azpilicueta (c) (James 55), Kante, Kovacic (Jorginho 106), Alonso, Pulisic (Werner 73), Havertz, Mount (Lukaku 73)

Liverpool (4-3-3): Kelleher, Alexander-Arnold, Matip (Konate 91), Van Dijk, Robertson, Henderson (c) (Elliot 80), Fabinho, Keita (Milner 80), Salah, Mane (Jota 80), Diaz (Origi 97)

The build-up to the final was very sombre given the world news that Ukraine were under attack from Russia. In the world of football UEFA quickly announced that the Champions League Final would now be played at the Stade de France in Paris instead of St Petersburg in Russia. With the government looking to sanction Russian oligarchs, Roman Abramovich's name was not on the intial list, despite his name being spoken about a lot in the media.

Thomas Tuchel stated in his pre-Liverpool press conference; "We should not pretend that this isn't an issue. At the moment I would love to take my right not to comment on it, until there is a decision made. But we are aware of it and it is distracting and worrying us, and to a certain degree, I can understand the critical opinions towards the club and towards us who represent the club."

The night before the final Roman Abramovich released the following statement on the official website; "During my nearly 20-year ownership of Chelsea FC, I have always viewed my role as a custodian of the Club, whose job it is ensuring that we are as successful as we can be today, as well as build for the future, while also playing a positive role in our communities. I have always taken decisions with the Club's best interests at heart. I remain committed to these values. That is why I am today giving trustees of Chelsea's charitable Foundation the stewardship and care of Chelsea FC. I believe that currently they are in the best position to look after the interests of the Club, players, staff and fans."

In all honesty it left more questions to be asked rather than answers. The final itself was a huge match and a repeat of the 2005 final that was played on the same day. Like then I was going with my brother Steve although there was a strange feel to the day in light of what was happening in Ukraine. We decided to do what we would normally do on a Wembley day and meet at Baker Street. With The Globe pub always packed with Chelsea fans we decided to go there. The doors weren't opening until 11:30am and at 10:45am there was already Chelsea fans gathering outside whilst the flags were being put up on the outside railings.

The club had also released another statement in the morning on the official website; "The situation in Ukraine is horrific and devastating. Chelsea FC's thoughts are with everyone in Ukraine. Everyone at the club is praying for peace".

The atmosphere inside and outside The Globe was fantastic with many new and old songs being belted out with all to see and hear. As always it was great to see and catch up with some familiar faces from Twitter. As we knew it was going to be a long day, me and Steve said we'd go for a pizza and then go back to the pub before getting the tube. Once we'd got in the restaurant Steve instantly bought a bottle of champagne. Although it's been the norm over the last 20 years of Chelsea reaching finals, we have always had the thought process of never taking any trophy for granted.

Back to The Globe and it was apparent it was clearing out so we only stayed for one drink before getting the tube. As we all pilled on the next available Metropolitan line it was full of Chelsea fans in fine voice all the way to Wembley Park. The nerves certainly kicked in as we walked down Wembley way. Despite it being a very difficult game there was a huge boost knowing Tuchel had a strong squad to pick from only missing Ben Chilwell and Hakim Ziyech.

We were fortunate to have lower tier tickets in Block 115 but it has to be said I thought the atmosphere sounded fantastic throughout the whole Chelsea end. The match itself was a great spectacle with both teams really going for it. Liverpool had chances with Edouard Mendy making some fantastic saves and also had a goal ruled out by VAR for offside. Mason Mount had two glorious chances for Chelsea and he would know he should've scored them. Over the 120 minutes we had three goals chalked off for offside with Lukaku's being the most controversial of all. There's also no doubt that in the second-half Naby Keita should have got his marching orders after a poor high foul on Trevoh Chalobah, who after the game needed stitches. The game was to be decided by penalties but on reflection I felt we deserved to win it and were unfortunate with some big decisions going against us. Nethertheless a very good competitive team performance.

Kepa, who had been outstanding for Chelsea throughout the whole competition, came on at the end of extra-time for the penalty shoot-out. Liverpool won the toss and the penalties were taken in front of their fans. The quality of penalties were excellent and every outfield player scored before the goalkeepers had to step up. Kelleher scored his so all eyes were now on Kepa. He blazed far over the bar and unfortunately that was it.

Despite the loss there was a feeling of pride and we really couldn't have put in a better performance.

MARCH 2022

2nd March
F.A Cup 5th Round
Luton Town 2-3 Chelsea
Kenilworth Road
Attendance: 10,140

Chelsea (3-4-3): Kepa, Rudiger, Loftus-Cheek, Sarr, Hudson-Odoi (Vale 63), Jorginho (c) (James 76), Saul, Kenedy (Pulisic 63), Mount, Lukaku, Werner
Chelsea Goals: Saul (27), Werner (68), Lukaku (78)

Luton Town (3-5-2): Steer (Isted 14), Burke, Lockyer, Potts (c), Kioso, Berry (Campbell 63), Osho, Mendes Gomes (Hylton 76), Bell, Cornick (Jerome 63), Muskwe (Snodgrass 76)
Luton Town Goals: Burke (2), Cornick (40)

With the questions Thomas Tuchel was asked during his pre-match press conference you'd be forgiven for thinking there wasn't even a game he was preparing for. At one stage he became a little frustrated but handled himself very well as he had done throughout the season; "Listen, STOP asking me these questions. I'm not a politician!"

There was plenty of noise around Chelsea at this time, with many having strong opinions without knowing anything factual. Just an hour before the game against Luton the club made another statement directly from owner Roman Abramovich; "I would like to address the speculation in the media over the past few days in relation to my ownership of Chelsea FC. As I have always taken decisions with the Club's best interest at heart. In

94

the current situation, I have therefore taken the decision to sell the Club, as I believe this is in the best interest of the Club, the fans, the employees, as well as the Club's sponsors and partners.

The sale of Club will not be fast-tracked but will follow due process. I will not be asking for any loans to be repaid. This has never been about business nor money for me, but about pure passion for the game and Club. Moreover, I have instructed my team to set up a charitable foundation where all proceeds from the sale will be donated. The foundation will be for the benefit of all victims of the war in Ukraine. This included providing critical funds towards the urgent and immediate needs of victims, as well as supporting the long-term work of recovery.

Please know this has been an incredibly difficult decision to make, and it pains me to part with the Club in this manner. However, I do believe this is in the best interest of the Club.

I hope that I will be able to visit Stamford Bridge one last time to say goodbye to all of you in person. It has been a privilege of a lifetime to be part of Chelsea FC and I am proud of all our joint achievements. Chelsea Football Club and its supporters will always be in my heart.

Thank you,
Roman"

A really sad and emotional statement to read and a real shame it had ended the way it had. The statement sent shockwaves around the footballing world, with real uncertainty surrounding what the future held for the Club. Since Roman arrived at Chelsea in 2003 he literally made our wildest dreams come true.

The Club and supporters had to now instantly focus on the match which was undoubtly hard. A Championship club away from home in a tight ground and big atmosphere. Thomas Tuchel made the changes to his team selection and in came Saul, Kenedy and the biggest surprise was Loftus-Cheek as a centre back.

The game couldn't have started any worse as we found ourselves 1-0 down after just two minutes from a corner. Saul scored a great equaliser with his first Chelsea goal but Luton regained the lead shortly before half-time after some poor defending.

It really felt it was going to be one of those dreadful days supporting Chelsea but Timo Werner scored our second equaliser with a great first touch and finish. Timo turned provider ten minutes later for Romelu Lukaku to tap-in. It was far from a great performance but in the circumstances it was an important victory.

Thomas Tuchel stated after the match; "It's big news and will be big change, but I am also never afraid of change and I'll focus on what I can influence".

5th March
Premier League
Burnley 0-4 Chelsea
Turf Moor
Attendance: 19,439

Chelsea (3-4-3): Mendy, Chalobah, Thiago Silva, Rudiger, James (Loftus-Cheek 71), Kante (Kovacic 71), Jorginho (c), Saul, Pulisic, Havertz, Mount (Werner 78)
Chelsea Goals: James (48), Havertz (53, 55), Pulisic (69)

Burnley (4-4-2): Pope, Roberts, Tarkowski (c), Collins, Taylor, Lennon, Westwood, Brownhill, McNeil, Rodriguez (Cornet 64), Weghorst (Barnes 78)

The talk of Chelsea was all about potential new owners with no solid facts, or clarity as to whether Roman Abramovich would have his assets frozen by the UK government.

Conor Gallagher and Edouard Mendy won the Young Player and Goalkeeper Of The Year at the London Footballer Of The Year awards and Paulo Ferreira left his role as loan player technical coach which ended a nearly 20 year stay at Chelsea. The draw was also made for F.A Cup quarter-finals and Chelsea would face Championship side Middlesbrough at the Riverside Stadium. 25 years on from when the two sides met in the final at Wembley.

Despite all the rumours and speculation around the sale of Chelsea FC Thomas Tuchel said in his pre-match Burnley press conference, "Chelsea, for me, is a perfect fit. I love to be here. I love everything about the club. Hopefully it continues. I am positive, I hope things will end well".

Chelsea were wearing the third kit at Burnley which was the first time we'd worn it all season in the Premier League. The F.A agreed leading up to the match that Chelsea could continue to have a Club World Cup badge in the centre of the shirt.

Despite Burnley's struggles in the Premier League this felt like a potentially difficult game. It showed in the first-half with The Blues only having one shot on target and relying on Thiago Silva to clear off the line. The second-half was a completely different story that saw Chelsea go on a rampage. Reece James was making his first start in almost ten weeks and opened the scoring emphatically with a well-hit shot into the corner after twisting and turning.

Just five minutes later Kai Havertz scored two goals in two minutes to completely kill the game. A great header from a perfect Christian Pulisic cross and then a close-range finish from a terrific ball from Reece James. It was soon 4-0 with a tidy finish from the lurking Christian Pulisic after a defensive mix up. Despite all the noise surrounding the club this was a really good result and second-half performance. Kai Havertz was really showing good form and the returning Reece James was a real boost. Chelsea made it three successive league wins for the first time since October.

10th March
Premier League
Norwich City 1-3 Chelsea
Carrow Road
Attendance: 26,722

Chelsea (3-4-3): Mendy, Chalobah, Thiago Silva, Christensen, Azpilicueta (c) (Loftus-Cheek h/t), Jorginho, Kovacic (Kante 85), Saul, Mount, Havertz, Werner (Lukaku 85)

Chelsea Goals: Chalobah (3), Mount (14), Havertz (90)

Norwich City (3-3-2-2): Krul, Zimmermann (Rupp h/t), Hanley (c), Kabak, Aarons, Lees-Melou, Normann (Rashica h/t), McLean, Williams, Sargent (Rowe 83), Pukki
Norwich City Goal: Pukki (69 pen)

A Thursday night trip to East Anglia for Chelsea in a re-arranged fixture. Images coming from Cobham a couple of days before was that of Ben Chilwell in light training for the first time since his injury with the ball at his feet.

Thomas Tuchel announced in his pre-match press conference that Reece James had a muscle injury on his other leg, unrelated to his previous injury. A real blow as he reminded everyone of his quality against Burnley. Tuchel also added his thoughts on the likely departure of Andreas Christensen at the end of the season. "It is in doubt, no? We hear the rumours and the situation with Andreas, since many weeks, is clear and we are not happy about it. Personally and club representatives think it's best for him to stay." Fans were also frustrated that with the Middlesbrough F.A Cup tie being a 5:30pm kick-off there would be no returning trains to London after the game.

On the day of the Norwich game I woke to everyone's posts on social media celebrating the 117th birthday of Chelsea Football Club. Returning home from the school run the news broke. Roman Abramovich was sanctioned by the UK Government, with all his assets frozen, which would bar the sale of Chelsea Football Club. The news had sent the club and the supporters into absolute chaos. The future was unknown, with many conflicting stories. Chelsea could still operate under a special licence. The club would continue to play matches and receive broadcast money but not be allowed to sell any more tickets or official merchandise. Only season ticket holders could go to games for the foreseeable future, with restrictions on how much the club could spend on home and away matchdays including travel and accommodation.

Government sanctions also stated that we couldn't buy new players and the club could only be sold if Abramovich allowed the

UK Government to take control of the process and received no proceeds from the sale.

Shortly before kick-off a spokesperson for 'Three UK' said; "In light of the government's recently announced sanctions, we have requested Chelsea Football Club temporarily suspend our sponsorship of the club, including the removal of our brand from shirts and around the stadium until further notice.

We recognise that this decision will impact the many Chelsea fans who follow their team passionately. However, we feel that given the circumstances, and the Government sanction that is in place, it is the right thing to do.

As a mobile network, the best way we can support the people of Ukraine is to ensure refugees arriving in the UK from the conflict and customers currently in Ukraine can stay connected to the people who matter to them. Therefore, we are offering connectivity packages to all Ukrainians arriving in the UK, and those in Ukraine."

Despite all the uncertainty Chelsea started the game in emphatic style. Trevoh Chalobah scoring a great header from a Mason Mount corner after just three minutes. Things got even better for The Blues when Mason Mount scored a terrific goal and proceeded to run to the away fans whilst kissing the badge.

It felt at this stage we could go on to score plenty more like we did at Stamford Bridge earlier on in the season. Despite many chances it didn't happen and in the second-half we gave Norwich a lifeline. Pukki pulled one back from the penalty spot with 20 minutes to go after Chalobah had handled the ball in the area. The points however were sealed in the final minute after a clever finish from the in-form Kai Havertz. A decent and much-needed win in one of the most strangest days in Chelsea history.

Thomas Tuchel stated after the game; "So far we can trust each other and this will not change. As long as we have enough shirts and a bus to drive to the games we will be there and will compete hard."

There was a lot of speculation as to what was happening and difficult to know exactly what was fact with very little being officially released. Sky Sports news reported that Chelsea's bank accounts had been temporarily seized by Barclays bank. Nike appeared committed to the long-term kit deal but Hyundai the club's sleeve sponsor followed Three by temporarily suspending the deal.

Hyundai: "In the current circumstances, we have taken the decision to suspend our marketing and communication activities with the Club until further notice."

Trivago however took a different approach; "We are looking forward to a transition of ownership as soon as possible and want to support the club in this process. We will provide any update to our business relationship if and when appropriate."

As the weekend approached it was reported that Roman Abramovich had given the green light for the club to be sold, with the UK Government also wanting a sale. There were a few names being mentioned but at this stage it was all media speculation. It was also urged by the Government for Chelsea supporters to refrain from chorusing support of Roman Abramovich during the Newcastle game. The day before the match it was announced that Chelsea's licence to operate had been amended by the Government, including the raising of the matchday budget for security, stewarding, services from £500,000 to 900,000. Also other provisions included those relating to expenses payable to parents of academy players.

The Premier League also made the following statement; "Following the imposition of sanctions by the UK Governement, the Premier League Board has disqualified Roman Abramovich as a Director of Chelsea Football Club.

The Board's decision does not impact on the club's ability to train and play it's fixtures, as set out under the terms of a licence issued by the Government which expires on 31 May 2022."

13th March
Premier League
Chelsea 1-0 Newcastle United
Stamford Bridge
Attendance: 40,026

Chelsea (4-3-3): Mendy, Chalobah, Christensen, Rudiger, Sarr

(Pulisic 78), Jorginho (c), Kante, Mount (Kovacic 63), Ziyech, Havertz, Werner (Lukaku 63)
Chelsea Goal: Havertz (89)

Newcastle United (3-4-3): Dubravka, Schar, Burn, Lascelles (c), Manquilo, S. Longtaff, Guimaraes, Targett, Almiron (Saint-Maximin 69), Wood, Murphy (Fraser 90)

A couple of weeks prior to the match me and my dad were unable to make the Newcastle game so sold our tickets to friends at face value. My circumstances changed and now I was desperate to go. On the Friday evening through some great friends on Twitter I managed to get myself a ticket. It was a game I just felt I needed to be at. A very strange feeling on the morning of the game and a realisation of what was happening to our great club. It wasn't helped with a disruptive mainline train service meaning a replacement bus service was in operation.

Being part of the Chelsea Supporters' Trust board we invited parts of the press to meet with us to discuss what we wanted for the future of our club amid speculation of many taking an interest in buying the club. As the rain came down interviews were taking place and our banner stated 'Trust In Our Future'. It was also good to meet up with Jason Cundy and his son James who although were working for Talk Sport had the same feelings as everyone else.

You couldn't even buy a programme on the day and it was sad to see the megastore closed which is usually buzzing on a match day. However, a new book edited by Mark Worrall called 'Tales From The Shed' was available to buy from the "cfcuk" stall which included 34 stories from Chelsea supporters which I was happy to contribute to. Proceeds going to our neighbours at Stoll Veterans co-inciding with the Big Stamford Bridge Sleep Out which was due to take place on March 26th. Along with the Peter Bonetti memorial there was still uncertainty at this point if these events would still go ahead in the circumstances.

Despite Three UK and Hyundai suspending their sponsorships with Chelsea their advertising hoardings remained around Stamford Bridge and on the player's shirts. It was thought in order to remove these further costs would be implemented and that was something we weren't allowed to do. Some fans proceeded to patch up their own shirts covering the sponsorships.

Petr Cech was interviewed prior to the match and said the club are operating "day by day" amid the ongoing restrictions, but was hopeful Thomas Tuchel would stay at the club. There was also a lot of talk about potential new owners but at this point it was only speculation and noise with many second guessing. Season Ticket holder and potential candidate to buy the club Nick Candy was interviewed by Sky Sports as he made his way to his seat. He stated, "I love Chelsea, I don't mind where it ends up, even if it's not with me, as long as it's in safe hands." He also mentioned how important it was to have supporter representation on the board.

Despite all the uncertainty the atmosphere inside Stamford Bridge was very good with many feeling that this could be their last match at Stamford Bridge for a while with restrictions at this point still stating no further tickets for matches were available, unless they'd been purchased before March 10th.

The banter between the Newcastle supporters and us was very humorous at times.

Newcastle fans: "Mike Ashley, he's coming for you...."

Chelsea fans response: "Boris Johnson, he's coming for you..."

It did make me laugh!

The game itself was far from a classic and in honesty for long periods it was quite a frustrating watch. Eddie Howe inevitably had Newcastle very well-drilled, organised and defending in numbers. We'd dropped many points at home this season it felt this could be another and despite our dominance in possession Newcastle were also getting chances.

One of the key talking points was whether Kai Havertz should have been sent off for the use of his elbow. It looked worse in the replays but it appeared he only had eyes for the ball despite it being a strong challenge. He only received a yellow card which I felt was the right decision. Trevoh Chalobah on the other hand was very fortunate not to give away a penalty. I was relieved as he was pulling the shirt of the Newcastle player and also fouled him. It once again showed the in inconsistencies of the officials using VAR. We've had plenty of decisions go against us this season but felt we got away with one here.

As we approached the end of the game it felt 0-0 was inevitable in a frustrating game. Kai Havertz had other ideas and saved the day for Chelsea in the 89th minute. A wonderful pass from Jorginho found Havertz who controlled and finished perfectly. The ground erupted with a blue flare going off in the Matthew Harding Lower stand. There was another chance for Havertz but he couldn't convert and with a header saved in the first-half he could have had a hat trick. One was enough and a massive three points. Jorginho added after the game; "We deserved the win. It was a great result, atmosphere and great for the fans."

Thomas Tuchel was asked in his post-match press conference about the complications around Chelsea travelling to Lille a few days later in the Champions League. "We can go by plane and come back by plane. If not, we'll go by train. If not, I'll drive a seven-seater. Honestly, I will do it. You can mark my words, I will do to arrive there."

16th March
Champions League, Last 16, Second-Leg
Lille 1-2 Chelsea (1-4 on agg)
Stade Pierre Mauroy
Attendance: 49,048

Chelsea (3-5-2): Mendy, Christensen (Chalobah 33), Thiago Silva, Rudiger, Azpilicueta (c), Kante, Jorginho (Loftus-Cheek 74), Kovacic (Mount h/t), Alonso, Havertz (Ziyech 83), Pulisic (Lukaku 74)
Chelsea Goals: Pulisic (45), Azpilicueta (72)

Lille (4-4-2): Jardim, Celik (Weah 59), Fonte (c), Botman (Onana 59), Djalo, Bamba (Gomes 78), Andre, Xeka, Gudmundsson (Bradaric 78), David (Ben Arfa 78), Yilmaz
Lille Goal: Yilmaz (38 pen)

Preparation for our second-leg against Lille was chaotic to say the least with again focus very much on everything apart from the football itself. It was starting to feel much of the media were coming at Chelsea very negatively and in parliament with less focus on the bigger issues. One of Chelsea's other sponsors MSC Cruises had joined Three UK and Hyundai in suspending their contract with the club. There was still plenty of speculation around potential buyers with official bids due on Friday March 18th. In all honesty the stories were changing all the time with many big media outlets providing conflicting news. Things would eventually be made much clearer.

Thomas Tuchel and Kai Havertz faced the media ahead of the game. Kai added when asked on paying for travel; "I would pay, no problem. That's not a big deal for us. To come to the games is the most important. There are harder moments in the world than taking the plane or bus to away games." Travel and accommodation had already been paid for before the sanctions came into place but arrangements around Middlesbrough away in the F.A Cup were proving a little more complicated.

Thomas Tuchel was asked about Boris Johnson's spokesperson telling Chelsea supporters to stop Abramovich chants. "I don't know if these are the most important subjects to talk about in parliament. If they are being discussed in parliament, maybe we need to worry about the priorities of discussion."

The day before the Lille game Chelsea released a statement that said unfortunately Chelsea supporters could still not purchase tickets for the away game against Middlesbrough. The supporters on the away scheme would still be allowed to attend as they had already been purchased, around 700 supporters. The club stated that in light of this they felt the game should be played behind closed doors. Inevitably this went down very badly and especially with Middlesbrough and rightly so. Quite frankly it was a ridiculous request and was later retracted.

Middlesbrough responded very quickly with chairman Steve Gibson stating; "I can't believe it. Sporting integrity and Chelsea do not belong in the same sentence. For 19 years corrupt money has fuelled Chelsea's success."

More sanctions were also imposed on Roman Abramovich from the European Union which initially threw the game itself into jeopardy. UEFA cleared up any concern about the fixture very quickly and the game would go ahead. Chelsea had a full allocation of support in Lille as tickets had already been purchased.

As kick-off edged closer UEFA announced that Chelsea would not be allowed to have supporters attend matches later in the competition until the club was sold. There were some unfortunate scenes in Lille, as a pub full of Chelsea supporters were tear gassed by the French police.

The game itself wasn't a classic and we made hard work for ourselves for long periods and there was a real moment of concern when Lille went 1-0 up through a penalty after Jorginho had handled. He soon made up for this with a sublime ball on the stroke of half-time for Christian Pulisic to finish well.

With 20 minutes remaining came the winning goal. Captain Cesar Azpilicueta met Mason Mount's left wing cross with his knee to ensure a 4-1 aggregate victory. Another very professional performance from Thomas Tuchel's team and now into the last eight. Joe Cole added on BT Sport after the game; "We've been through turbulent times and we've seen such poor examples of leadership throughout our society and to see a football manager step up like that, talking like that is a breath of fresh air. He should be Prime Minister."

There was also the birth of a new song on the night;

"We're on our way, we're on our way.
To Paris, we're on our way.
Seven-seater, car or train, Tommy's gonna fly the plane.
All I know is Chelsea's on their way".

19th March
F.A Cup Quarter-final
Middlesbrough 0-2 Chelsea
Riverside Stadium
Attendance: 31,422

Chelsea (4-3-3): Mendy, Azpilicueta (c), Thiago Silva, Rudiger, Sarr, Mount, Loftus-Cheek, Kovacic (Kante 69), Ziyech (Kenedy 81), Lukaku (Vale 84). Pulisic (Werner 68)
Chelsea Goals: Lukaku (15), Ziyech (31)

Middlesbrough (3-5-2): Lumley, Dijksteel, Fry (Bamba h/t), McNair (Peltier 53), Jones, Crooks, Howson, Tavernier, Taylor (Bola 58), Connolly (Watmore 58), Balogun (Coburn 74)

There wasn't much time for preparation for the trip to Middlesbrough but there was certainly plenty going on. Another sponsor suspended its contract with the club, this time it was Parimatch.

Gareth Southgate announced his latest England squad which included Reece James (who later withdrew through injury), Mason Mount, Conor Gallagher and former blues Tammy Abraham and Marc Guehi. Saul Niguez also announced on his instagram account that he had Covid-19.

The day before the match was a very busy one. There was a memorial at Stamford Bridge for club legend, Peter Bonetti. A wonderful service with many supporters in attendance located in the Shed End. Whilst on my way home I had a sense of realisation about our fantastic club and its history. Peter made 729 appearances in goal for Chelsea winning the League Cup, F.A Cup and the European Cup Winners' Cup.

It was also the quarter-final draw for the Champions League. Chelsea would face Spanish giants Real Madrid over two legs and if victorious play either Atletico Madrid or Manchester City in the semi-final stage. A difficult draw but we could take confidence in the fact that we'd beaten all three sides on the way to winning the Champions League just the season before.

It was also the day where all official bids for the club had to be submitted before 9pm. A huge day.

With no tickets on sale for Chelsea supporters there was only the supporters on the away scheme who could make the trip to Middlesbrough for the Saturday tea time kick-off. Around 700 travelling fans made plenty of noise but it should have been around 4,600.

The one's who did make the trip with awkward transport links were certainly not disappointed as Chelsea eased through to the semi-final. It was a potential banana skin cup tie but Tuchel put a strong team out and we dominated throughout the game. Lukaku opened the scoring after just 15 minutes from close-range after Mason Mount provided the perfect cross for Romelu to tap-in from close-range.

Birthday boy Hakim Ziyech made it 2-0 just after the half hour mark with a fantastic trademark left foot shot from distance after cutting in. There were no more goals but it never felt we were really under any threat and professionally saw the game out. Thiago Silva oozed class as he does so often and received the Man Of The Match award. Mason Mount had now been directly involved in 50 goals for Chelsea with 25 goals and 25 assists.

Chelsea were heading to Wembey but there was uncertainty about tickets. We would face Crystal Palace who hammered Everton, the other semi-final would be contested between Liverpool and Manchester City. There was now an international break for two weeks but the main topic in the sports world was that of the Chelsea takeover. All official bids were in but it was now up to the independent Raine Group to decide who would be on the short list. With a few prospective buyers making their cases public, there was also some that remained anonymous. It wasn't long for #NoToRicketts to start trending on Twitter with many venting their frustration towards the family, some of whom had made controversial statements in the past relating to equality and diversity. Even by Thursday March 24th there was still no official short list but plenty of rumours and conflicting reports. The Saudi Media group did however make it known they were out of the running but didn't rule out joining another consortium. It was all very confusing but did feel like we nearing more clarity with regards to an outcome.

Chelsea were given an update regarding the selling of tickets. Chelsea could sell tickets for the F.A Cup semi-final at Wembley, at home to Real Madrid and all away matches. However, we weren't allowed to sell tickets for home Premier League matches and only season ticket holders would be able to attend. The question on everyone's lips was, why? Away fans would also be able to attend matches at Stamford Bridge. This would not affect the capacity for the Brentford game at home as tickets were already purchased before the sanctions came in on March 10th. What made it even more strange was that the UK Government allowed Roman Abramovich to deposit £30m to the club to ensure they could continue to operate.

As the deadline of Friday came for the Chelsea takeover shortlist it still wasn't clarified who was actually on it and there was still a possibility that the ones who didn't make it could potentially join other consortiums that did.

Here's how journalists were reporting it over the weekend of 26th / 27th March.

'Martin Broughton's Chelsea bid, which includes Seb Coe, is seen as a particularly strong contender - and it was no surprise that it was shortlisted. The consortium is made up of global backers.'
James Robson – 'Standard Sport'

'The Bidding could go over £2.5BN with Chelsea wanting an extra £1BN+ guaranteed in a binding agreement for investment into Stamford Bridge and the squad to keep them competitive in the league and Champions league. (That's like £3.5BN+)'
Matt Law – 'Telegraph'

'The Ricketts family have already made it clear that they can meet Chelsea's financial demands but that may not be enough to win over supporters, whose views will be taken into consideration before a buyer is picked. The successful bidder will not be decided on the sale price alone and confirmation that the views of the Chelsea fans will be taken into consideration leaves the Ricketts family facing an uphill battle.

Chelsea and Raine will examine that relationship in greater detail during the final stage of the sale process.'
Matt Law – 'Telegraph'

'The four remaining contenders to buy Chelsea Football Club have been told they must commit at least £1BN to future investment in the Chelsea stadium and squad. It will be a contractual guarantee that the winning bidder must have an additional £1BN + Available for multiple areas of Chelsea.'
   'Sky News'

'A dramatic couple of days in the bid to buy Chelsea. We have a shortlist of four and Raine want the sale completed by the end of April. Now bidders get access to the the data room, which could see them lower offers or pull out, both of which are unlikely.'
   James Robson – 'Standard Sport'

   The Chelsea Supporters' Trust held the 'Big Stamford Bridge Sleep Out' on the 26th March with a number of supporters sleeping in the East Stand open aired concourse raising money for our neighbours at Stoll Veterans. A huge well done to all those that attended and donated.
   Although many international games were taking place across the globe including World Cup play-offs the news was predominately dominated by Will Smith smacking Chris Rock live on stage at the Oscars. With most only realising the event was taking place because of the incident.
   Further news reports regarding potential new owners;

'The mystery and uncertainty around the current ability of Pagliuca and Josh Harris's bid to complete a deal leaves Boehly as the frontrunner.'
   Matt Law – 'Telegraph'

'The deadline for final bids to purchase Chelsea from the groups shortlisted must be submitted on or around April 11th. What the Chelsea fans say in the last few weeks of the race will be heard in government and the louder they say it, the better.'
   Matt Law – 'Telegraph'

'Shortlisted bidders for Chelsea are permitted to make new and

improved bids. Two of the four known parties are ready to increase their offers.'
  Sami Mokbel – 'Daily Mail'

'Boehly and Broughton are the leading two contenders to buy Chelsea FC. Ricketts family do have a strong pitch, but they're so unpopular. To not listen to the fanbase when picking an owner would be damaging to the club.'
  Ben Jacobs – 'CBS Sports'

'An April 11th deadline for second bids. The chance to meet Chelsea department heads. A tour of the club's facilities. The aim of a sale by end of April. Shortlisted bidders have been given the green light to set up meetings with Chelsea officials and tours, which could start as early as this week.'
  Matt Law – 'Telegraph'

'Raine have confirmed to 'Telegraph Sport' that fan views will be taken into consideration during the final decision. Sources close to Stephen Pagliuca claim he is prevented from making public the details of his Chelsea bid by non-disclosure agreements. The mystery and uncertainty around the current ability of Pagliuca and Josh Harris's bid to complete a deal leaves Boehly as the frontrunner.
  Matt Law – 'Telegraph'

On Monday 28th March the 'Wall Street Journal' reported that Roman Abramovich had suffered suspected chemical weapons poisoning along with Ukraine peace negotiators earlier in the month. Further tickets were put on sale for supporters including Real Madrid, F.A Cup semi-final and Southampton away. Most notably from the international break was that Euro 2020 winners Italy failed to qualify for the World Cup after a shock last-minute defeat to North Macedonia.

APRIL 2022

2nd April
Premier League
Chelsea 1-4 Brentford
Stamford Bridge
Attendance: 39,061

Chelsea (4-3-3): Mendy, Azpilicueta (c), Thiago Silva, Rudiger, Alonso (James 56), Kante (Kovacic 65), Loftus-Cheek, Mount, Ziyech, Havertz, Werner (Lukaku 65)
Chelsea Goal: Rudiger (48)

Brentford (3-4-1-2): Raya, Ajer, Jansson (c), Pinnock, Roerslev, Norgaard, Janelt (Jensen 81), Henry (Canos 88), Eriksen, Mbeumo (Wissa 85), Toney
Brentford Goals: Janelt (50, 61), Eriksen (54), Wissa (87)

Leading up to the game the talk of social media was a protest against the Ricketts family who made the shortlist as they pursued a takeover. With many supporters questioning their morals regarding equality, diversity and inclusion the plan was for many to meet and express their concern outside Stamford Bridge on the day of the game at 12 noon. The Premier League also announced that five substitutes can be used from the start of the 2022/23 season. Still no sale of official match day programmes but issue 234 of the 'cfcuk' fanzine was released in time for the match.

As my dad couldn't make the match I took my boy Jack. His first experience of a Premier League match and just his second visit to Stamford Bridge after the Plymouth game in February. It was almost a year to the day that Chelsea suffered a shock 5-2 home defeat to West Bromwich Albion and this day had a very similar feeling.

It was our first home league defeat since September with the game certainly coming to life in the second-half. It started off an even affair but a nervous one from The Blues as Thomas Frank inevitably had his Brentford side very organised. At half-time I still felt we could go on and win the game and after the re-start Antonio Rudiger put us into the lead with a fantastic long-range strike. He was actually 39.6 yards out, that was Chelsea's longest range Premier League goal for over 15 years. Confidence grew from the Stamford Bridge crowd but it was very short lived. Brentford soon replied and scored three goals in just 11 minutes with a complete Chelsea collapse. Substitutions were made but it just wasn't our day with Brentford making it four shortly before the end. It was a lacklustre performance and it appeared Thomas Tuchel had underestimated the opposition and his tactics.

As for Jack he took defeat quite well in all honesty which was undoubtedly the worst performance of the season. He was insistent on staying to the final whistle whilst many poured out and he proceeded to say, "You can't win every game Daddy, you've been saying that to me for years". It's the defeats that make you stronger as a supporter, not the glory.

Whilst Tuchel questioned the lack of atmosphere around the ground, Thiago Silva took to Instagram; "Good days make you happy. Bad days bring you experience. Both are essential for life. Happiness makes you good, but troubles make you strong. Pain keeps you human, falls keep you humble. Success keeps you bright, but only GOD keeps you standing (Denzel Washington). WE keep going."

Next up was Real Madrid in the Champions League!

6th April
Champions League, Quarter-final, First-Leg
Chelsea 1-3 Real Madrid
Stamford Bridge
Attendance: 38,689
Chelsea (3-4-3): Mendy, Christensen (Kovacic h-t), Thiago Silva,

Rudiger, James, Kante (Ziyech h-t), Jorginho (Loftus-Cheek 64),
Azpilicueta (c), Mount, Havertz, Pulisic (Lukaku 64)
Chelsea Goal: Havertz (40)

Real Madrid (4-3-3): Courtois, Carvajal, Militao (Nacho 64),
Alaba, Mendy, Kroos (Camavinga 74), Casemiro, Modric,
Valverde (Ceballos 86), Benzema (c) (Bale 86), Vinicius Junior
Real Madrid Goals: Benzema (21, 24, 46)

A game that just couldn't be missed! Out of all the games that
were played behind closed doors due to Covid-19 last season the
one that really hurt was the semi-final against Real Madrid in the
Champions League. A fixture that hasn't happened enough over
the years and if you weren't in Athens in 1971 or Monaco in 1998
it would be your first of seeing us play the Spanish giants. Me and
dad were buzzing for the game despite the £71 price per ticket
and an additional £2 booking fee.

Eden Hazard was injured but we would see manager Carlo
Ancelotti return and former goal keeper Thibaut Courtois who'd
inevitably get plenty of stick. A meal at Fulham Broadway with me
and dad discussing some of the best Champions League
knockout games we've witnessed over the years. Strangely
Brugge in 1995 and Vicenza 1998 came up despite those being in
the Cup Winners' Cup. Regardless, these European nights at
Stamford Bridge are special with great anticipation. Usually one of
those occasions where supporters would buy a match day
programme to mark the tie but these weren't even available in the
hospitality sections.

The atmosphere pre-match inside Stamford Bridge was
electric with the guys from 'We Are The Shed' unveiling a fantastic
mosaic to mark the club's recent Champions League success.

The game itself was an incredibly frustrating one with Real
having a great early chance with only the cross bar saving us. It
wasn't long after that two quick goals gave us a mountain to climb.
Two world class headers from Karim Benzema left us in complete
shock. With supporters looking at who was at fault sometimes you
just have to admire and accept the quality of some of the world's

best although feeling very dejected. What was also disappointing was the number of Real fans in the West Stand Lower causing many issues when the goals went in. Five minutes before half-time we had a lifeline. A fantastic cross from Jorginho found the in-form Kai Havertz who bravely headed past Courtois. At the break I was feeling very optimistic that we could kick on in the second-half as despite their lead Real looked fragile at times and we'd certainly be in the ascendency now we had a goal back.

Kovacic and Ziyech came on for Christensen and Kante but the second-half couldn't have started any worse. As many supporters were coming back up the stairs to their seats Edouard Mendy collected a long pass out of his area under little pressure but his square pass was short to Rudiger. Benezema intercepted and finished with ease. Just 45 seconds into the half and we were now 3-1 down. The referee didn't help our cause throughout the match but we couldn't blame him for world class finishing and an individual error. Romelu Lukaku came on with 25 minutes remaining and had two glorious headed chances but couldn't get them on target. A very frustrating night with it all to do in the return leg. Two disappointing home defeats but a night remembered for the class of Karim Benzema.

Thomas Tuchel was clearly frustrated after the match and said; "If we keep on playing like this we will lose in Southampton and then we don't need to think about the Bernabeu, we will get hammered".

9th April
Premier League
Southampton 0-6 Chelsea
St Mary's Stadium
Attendance: 31,359

Chelsea (3-5-2): Mendy, Christensen, Thiago Silva (James 63), Rudiger, Loftus-Cheek, Kante (c), Mount (Ziyech 69), Kovacic, Alonso, Havertz (Pulisic h-t), Werner
Chelsea Goals: Alonso (8), Mount (16, 54), Werner (21, 49), Havertz (31)

Southampton (4-3-1-2): Forster, Livramento (Smallbone 73), Bednarek, Salisu, Walker-Peters, Ward-Prowse (c), Romeu (Valery 36), S Armstrong, Elyounoussi, A Armstrong (Diallo h-t), Adams

A quick turnaround and it was back to Premier League action for the Saturday, 3pm kick-off on the south coast. With not much time inbetween there was nothing much of news, only that the official Chelsea v Real Madrid programmes were fetching between £60 - £70 on eBay and Mason Mount had finally got a haircut!

The line-up caused plenty of conversation on social media an hour before the match. With Azpilicueta out with Covid-19, Alonso came in at left wing-back with Loftus-Cheek on the right as Reece James was on the bench. Timo Werner returned to the starting line-up. On a day where we desperately needed to find some form the players certainly didn't disappoint as it was raining goals!

Marcos Alonso opened the scoring on eight minutes with a low drive after a great assist from Mason Mount. It was soon 2-0 with a ferocious shot from outside the box from Mason. Werner then added a third before Havertz made it four with only half an hour played. At half-time you could be forgiven thinking we could get double figures. Kai Havertz came off at half-time and was replaced by Pulisic. Just four minutes after the restart Werner scored his second and Chelsea's fifth with a great solo effort. He was having a great game with two goals and striking the woodwork three times in the match. Mason Mount scored his second just five minutes later with a tap-in and despite other chances the game finished 6-0 with Chelsea matching their highest ever away win in the Premier League. It was now our seventh successive away win, also equalling a club record.

In other Premier League news, Frank Lampard's Everton got a vital win in their relegation battle beating Manchester United 1-0 at Goodison Park. Arsenal lost at home to Brighton and title contenders Manchester City and Liverpool fought out a 2-2 draw at The Etihad Stadium with City just one point ahead. Chelsea remained third, five points clear of fifth-placed Tottenham with Chelsea having a game in hand. Surprisingly though Chelsea were fourth on Match Of The Day despite the rampant performance. All eyes were now firmly on Madrid.

12th April
Champions League, Quarter-final, Second-Leg
Real Madrid 2-3 Chelsea (AET) (5-4 on agg)
Bernabeu
Attendance: 59,839

Chelsea (3-4-1-2): Mendy, James, Thiago Silva, Rudiger, Loftus-Cheek (Saul 106), Kante (c) (Ziyech 99), Kovacic (Jorginho 106), Alonso, Mount, Havertz, Werner (Pulisic 83)
Chelsea Goals: Mount (15), Rudiger (51), Werner (75)

Real Madrid (4-3-3): Courtois, Carvajal, Nacho (Lucas Vazquez 88), Alaba, Mendy (Marcelo 78), Kroos (Camavinga 73), Casemiro (Rodrygo 78), Modric, Valverde, Benzema (c), Vinicius Junior (Ceballos 115)
Real Madrid Goals: Rodrygo (80), Benzema (96)

Leading up to the game prospective buyer of Chelsea Football Club Stephen Pagiluca finally broke his silence on buying the club and was at the previous match at Southampton. The statement like many of the others was stating the obvious things supporters wanted to hear. Thursday 14th April was the deadline for all final bids for prospective buyers who had already made the shortlist.

A huge game awaited with only a small amount of belief after the first-leg. Due to maintenance work on the ground only 1,800 tickets were allocated to Chelsea supporters in the Bernabeu. Me and my dad decided to go to the pub to watch the game feeling more hopeful than confident of a comeback. Thomas Tuchel added in his pre-match press conference; " Everything is still possible, but let's be realistic. It is still Bernabeu and there is a crowd and an opponent very different to Southampton. The task is huge. We are always up for a competition, we will try to win".

Many had written Chelsea off in the press going into the second-leg but Thomas Tuchel and the team had other ideas. We started the game on the front foot and Mason Mount got us off to the perfect start with a great side-foot finish after just 15 minutes. Reece James had also picked up an unluckly early yellow card but that certainly didn't affect his performance. Benzema had a couple of first-half chances but nothing to really affect how dominant and organised Chelsea were. At half-time I was very happy and thought we had every chance to continue the fight back.

Antonio Rudiger levelled the tie six minutes into the second-half after a fantastic header from a corner. We were in the ascendancy at this point and it looked like we'd continue to dominate. Marcos Alonso soon after rifled the ball into the top corner only for VAR to rule out for handball. A really silly rule as it had no impact on how the ball fell and the exquisite finish. There was however nothing to stop Timo Werner who did make it 3-0 after a wonderful solo effort with 15 minutes remaining.

Despite our dominance and incredible comeback just five minutes later Madrid scored through Rodrygo after a sensational ball from Modric on the outside of his boot. Substitute Christian Pulisic had two great chances to win it for Chelsea towards the end but couldn't convert. I'd actually had a bet before the game, Chelsea to win 4-1 and Mason Mount to score first. With odds of 200/1 I was inches away from this happening.

The tie went into extra-time and despite the continued effort and commitment you could see there was some tired legs out there and that showed just five minutes in. Benzema scored his fourth goal of the tie and another header after an unfortunate slip from Rudiger who amongst others was fantastic on the night. Ziyech, Havertz and Jorginho all had chances to take the tie to penalties but it just wasn't meant to be. Frustrations grew on the Chelsea bench with Madrid's time-wasting antics and Tuchel and Azpilicueta were both shown yellow cards.

Unfortunately it ended in defeat for Chelsea but it was certainly a performance to be proud of. Me and my dad reflected at full-time in the pub and couldn't fault the team's performance giving it absolutely everything. It was always going to be a mountain to climb but the damage was really done at Stamford Bridge in the first-leg. Chelsea were the first English team to score three goals at Real Madrid since 1968. Despite the aggregate defeat Chelsea made it eight away wins in a row which was a new club record.

17th April
F.A Cup Semi-final
Chelsea 2-0 Crystal Palace
Wembley Stadium
Attendance: 76,238

Chelsea (3-4-3): Mendy, James, Christensen (Thiago Silva 82), Rudiger, Azpilicueta (c), Jorginho (Kante 77), Kovacic (Loftus-Cheek 26), Alonso, Mount (Ziyech 77), Havertz (Lukaku 77), Werner
Chelsea Goals: Loftus-Cheek (65), Mount (76)

Crystal Palace (3-4-1-2): Butland, Koutate (Milivojevic 85), Anderson, Guehi, Ward, McArthur (c) (Olise 72), Schlupp (Benteke 72), Mitchell, Eze, Mateta (Ayew 55), Zaha

According to 'Standard Sport', Raine Group planned to present their choice of the new Chelsea owner to the UK Government in the week commencing April 18th, when a licence for sale will then be drawn up to complete the takeover. On Thursday April 14th the four consortia had to submit their final offers to buy the club. On Good Friday the Ricketts Family officially withdrew their final bid, much to the delight of many Chelsea supporters.

Easter Sunday saw Chelsea heading to Wembley in our only remaining cup competition. With many different views as to why Chelsea had struggled to sell out the full capacity for this fixture, possibly due to it being Easter weekend, train disruptions or the fact (and no disrespect) it was Crystal Palace. Chelsea had previously rejected Crystal Palace's request to play on loan midfielder Conor Gallagher. The media really got hold of this story and I found it strange so much was made of it. He's a Chelsea player so why on earth would we want him to potentially knock us out of the competition. Very rarely do loan players play against their contracted clubs so I couldn't understand why anyone would think this situation would be any different. Social media also went into meltdown when it was announced Anthony Taylor would referee the match. Inevitably we were favourites going into the game.

The first-half was very forgetful in what was a very dull encounter especially compared to the semi-final the day before which ended in a 3-2 victory for Liverpool. The only thing of significance was Mateo Kovacic going off injured midway through the first-half and being replaced by Ruben Loftus-Cheek. A real blow.

Chelsea began to dominate the game in the second-half and the breakthrough finally came with 25 minutes remaining. It was Ruben Loftus-Cheek who scored his first Chelsea goal in three years with a great half volley into the top corner via a slight deflection. Mason Mount soon ensured Chelsea would be back at Wembley on May 14th. A good interchange with Timo Werner saw Mount slot home with class and score his fourth goal in his last three games.

Crystal Palace put up a good fight and frustrated us at times but we came through in the end and booked a second domestic cup final with Liverpool. It was Chelsea's 54th game of the season in all competitions. By reaching the F.A Cup Final Chelsea would play 63 games this season with the only fixtures missing being the Champions League semi-finals and final. A great achievement.

20th April
Premier League
Chelsea 2-4 Arsenal
Stamford Bridge
Attendance: 32,249

Chelsea (3-4-1-2): Mendy, James, Christensen (Thiago Silva h-t), Sarr, Azpilicueta (c), Loftus-Cheek, Kante, Alonso (Ziyech 81), Mount, Lukaku (Havertz 60), Werner
Chelsea Goals: Werner (17), Azpilicueta (32)

Arsenal (3-4-3): Ramsdale, White, Holding, Gabriel, Saka, Elneny, Xhaka, Tavares, Odegaard, Nketiah (Martinelli 70), Smith Rowe (Soares 75)
Arsenal Goals: Nketiah (13, 57), Smith Rowe (27), Saka (pen 90)

This was Chelsea's first game where the government sanctions affected the capacity with only season ticket holders and away supporters allowed to attend. Heading to Stamford Bridge I felt quite confident as we looked to pull away from Arsenal in the race to finish in the top four places. Arsenal were in poor form having lost their previous three games. Despite my confidence we've all seen it before, when we make it very difficult for ourselves against them, despite being a better team.

This game unfortunately was no different. It was a rare occasion where Thomas Tuchel was at fault with a very questionable team selection that felt very much like a Carabao Cup starting 11. Andreas Christensen gifted Arsenal the lead with a very poor backpass but we soon responded through a deflected shot from Timo Werner. Smith Rowe put Arsenal in the lead with a clever shot but captain Azpilicueta equalised to make it 2-2 before half-time. It was a very entertaining game with some poor defending but it was certainly end to end. At the break I naively thought we'd go on to secure three points but it went from bad to worse.

Nketiah scored his second of the night after the ball bounced off our defenders and Saka secured victory from the spot after a foul from Azpilicueta. It really was one of those nights to forget as we looked over shoulder with the chasing pack edging nearer to us. Azpilicueta confronted angry supporters at the end of the game as tensions rose. It was the first time Chelsea had lost three home games in a row since 1993. We had also conceded 4+ goals for two consecutive league games for the first time since 1989.

24th April
Premier League
Chelsea 1-0 West Ham United

Stamford Bridge
Attendance: 32,231

Chelsea (3-4-1-2): Mendy, Chalobah, Thiago Silva, Azpilicueta (c), Loftus-Cheek (Ziyech 76), Kante, Jorginho, Alonso, Mount, Havertz (Lukaku 76), Werner (Pulisic 76)
Chelsea Goal: Pulisic (90)

West Ham United (3-4-3): Fabianski, Johnson, Dawson, Cresswell, Coufal, Soucek, Noble (c) (Rice 62), Masuaka, Yarmolenko (Bowen 73), Fornals, Benrahma (Lanzini 78)

Leading up to yet another London derby former Chelsea legend Didier Drogba was inducted into the Premier League Hall of Fame. Regarding the takeover, multiple sources reported that Serena Williams and Lewis Hamilton had agreed to invest millions of pounds in the takeover bid which was being led by Sir Martin Broughton.

I couldn't make the West Ham game as it was my daughter's birthday so my brother and dad attended. It had a real feel of an end of season game in honesty. Bright sunshine but there was a real lack of atmosphere and quality on the pitch. West Ham had defensive injuries and rested many key players as they looked ahead to their Europa League semi-final. Chelsea had players out including Mateo Kovacic and Reece James due to injuries. Thiago Silva was now officially the oldest outfield player to appear for Chelsea in the Premier League era.

Throughout the match we had to be patient although our build-up play was too slow at times. West Ham had a few half chances mainly due to our own individual errors but with just minutes remaining we were awarded a penalty after substitute Romelu Lukaku was brought down by Dawson, who was subsequently shown a red card. Jorginho stepped up and his tame effort was easily saved after a hop, skip and a jump. To be fair Jorginho's record in taking penalties this season had been very good but when his technique goes wrong it looks pretty awlful.

However, we kept looking for that winner and it finally came in injury time when Christian Pulisic swept in Marcos Alonso's cut back. A wonderful moment and a very important three points. In Thomas Tuchel's post-match press conference he confirmed Antonio Rudiger had spoken to him and expressed his desire to leave Stamford Bridge for Real Madrid at the end of the season. A very disappointing situation as he had been nothing short of exceptional since Tuchel arrived at the club.

28th April
Premier League
Manchester United 1-1 Chelsea
Old Trafford
Attendance: 73,564

Chelsea (3-4-1-2): Mendy, Azpilicueta (c), Thiago Silva, Rudiger, James, Kante (Loftus-Cheek 82), Jorginho, Alonso, Mount, Havertz (Lukaku 70), Werner (Pulisic 71)
Chelsea Goal: Alonso (60)

Manchester United (4-2-3-1): De Gea, Dalot, Lindelof, Varane, Telles, Matic (Jones 79), McTominay, Rashford (Mata 79), Fernandes, Elanga (Garnacho 75), Ronaldo
Manchester United Goal: Ronaldo (62)

Leading up to the match it seemed we edging nearer to the sale of the club with three consortiums in the running. It was reported by multiple sources that Roman Abramovich wanted the new owners to put up a further £500m for the club to be donated to charity.

A rearranged fixture saw Chelsea head to Old Trafford on a Thursday night in another important Premier League clash. Manchester United were going into this off two league defeats and our form was inconsistent to say the least. We had a great record at Old Trafford in the 1990's but now we seemed to find it incredibly difficult and not winning there since 2013. With Everton away to follow soon after this was a very big game.

Team news was interesting and barring Marcos Alonso in for

Ben Chilwell it was the same team that started the 2021 Champions League Final. Cesar Azpilicueta was also captaining Chelsea for the 200th time, a fantastic achievement.

Chelsea were dominant throughout the first-half and in all honesty it summed up much of our season. Plenty of good possession and chances created but lacking that cutting edge in front of goal. Kai Havertz had a couple of great chances to put us in front but we went into the break goalless much to the visible frustration of Thomas Tuchel. The second-half was very much the same but on the hour mark a cross from Reece James was headed on by Kai Havertz into the path of Alonso who volleyed emphatically on his left foot into the corner.

Finally we had a breakthrough but the lead lasted less than two minutes. A clever ball from former blue Nemanja Matic found Cristiano Ronaldo who wasn't going to miss, his first Premier League goal against Chelsea. Matic was actually fortunate to stay on the pitch after a stamp on Reece James who was having a fantastic game. It ended in a draw and left us feeling very frustrated as there was no doubt we should have won the game against a poor United team. Our supporters who made the trip were fantastic throughout making their voices heard. We were now six points clear of fourth place with five league games remaining. Three at home and two away, starting with a trip to Goodision Park and being reunited with Frank Lampard.

MAY 2022

1st May
Premier League
Everton 1-0 Chelsea
Goodison Park
Attendance: 39,256

Chelsea (3-4-1-2): Mendy, Azpilicueta (c) (Pulisic 68), Thiago Silva, Rudiger, James, Loftus-Cheek, Jorginho (Kovacic h-t), Alonso, Mount, Havertz, Werner (Ziyech 68)

Everton (5-4-1): Pickford, Iwobi, Coleman (c), Mina, Holgate, Mykolenko, Gordon, Doucoure, Delph (Allan 71), Gray (Alli 90), Richarlison (Rondon 80)
Everton Goal: Richarlison (47)

The day before the match there was some interesting news regarding the takeover of the club, with a dramatic late bid by Britain's richest man, Sir Jim Ratcliffe. Considering Raine had already conducted a shortlist it was certainly a surprise however there was much going on behind the scenes that many of us didn't know. Despite the late attempt it was thought by multiple sources that a consortium led by LA Dodgers owner Todd Boehly was the preferred bidder.

The night before the game Everton supporters proceeded to let off fireworks outside the Chelsea team hotel during the early hours which apparently lasted for half an hour. Our record at Goodison Park in recent seasons had been abysmal and no doubt they were going to be up for this one as their Premier League status was in serious jeopardy.

On reflection neither side looked capable of scoring in the first 45 minutes with very little to report. Just one minute into the second-half Everton scored after an individual error from Azpilicueta allowed Richarlison to finish well. We certainly had chances with Mason Mount hitting the woodwork and Jordan Pickford making some outstanding saves to deny Azpilicueta, Rudiger, Loftus-Cheek and Mateo Kovacic. It wasn't our day and we couldn't compete with a very physical Everton team who appeared to want it more. Our form was worrying as Arsenal had cut the gap to just three points as they won at West Ham. Tottenham were also continuing to fight for the top four after comfortably beating Leicester. Improvements were needed, we now had four games remaining with three of these at Stamford Bridge.

Frank Lampard stated after the match; "I have so much respect for Chelsea and the fans. So I hope they understand me getting excited with the win. We needed it more than them." Ruben Loftus-Cheek said, "We want top four but we cannot perform like that with other teams doing well around us. We need wins. It is hard to process it right now and we will look back at it once the emotions have calmed down."

7th May
Premier League
Chelsea 2-2 Wolverhampton Wanderers
Stamford Bridge
Attendance: 32,190

Chelsea (3-4-1-2): Mendy, Azpilicueta (c), (Sarr 87), Thiago Silva, Rudiger, James, Loftus-Cheek, Kovacic, Alonso (Saul h-t), Pulisic, Lukaku (Havertz 90), Werner
Chelsea Goals: Lukaku (56 pen, 58)

Wolverhampton Wanderers (3-5-2): Sa, Boly, Coady (c), Saiss (Chiquinho 70), Jonny, Dendoncker, Neves (Trincao 77), Moutinho, Ait-Nouri, Jimenez, Neto (Hwang 70)
Wolverhampton Wanderers Goals: Trincao (79), Coady (90)

There was no midweek action for Chelsea after the Everton game for the first time in a long while. However throughout the week there was plenty of things going regarding the takeover. The Times reported that the sale of the club had hit a serious obstacle over fears that Roman Abramovich wanted the £1.5bn loan repaid. However other reports suggested Roman expected the loan to be frozen on the club's sale and the government sanctions prevent him from writing the loan off as planned. As previously mentioned there were plenty of conflicting stories with some focusing on the worst possible scenarios which inevitably created the most appealing headlines. At this stage Sir Jim Ratcliffe did not appear to be put off trying to buy the club despite the consortium led by Todd Boehly being the clear favourite.

On May 5th a spokesperson for Roman Abramovich released a the following statement on the official Chelsea website responding to reports.

"Firstly, Mr Abramovich's intentions in relation to gifting the proceeds from the Chelsea sale to charity have not changed.

Since the initial announcement, Mr Abramovich's team has identified senior representatives from UN bodies and large global charitable organizations who have been tasked with forming a Foundation and setting out a plan for its activities. The lead independent expert has had conversations with Government representatives presenting the structure and initial plans.

Mr Abramovich has not been involved in this work and it has been managed independently by experts with years of experience working in humanitarian organizations.

Secondly, Mr Abramovich has not asked for any loan to be repaid to him – such suggestions are entirely false – as are suggestions that Mr Abramovich increased the price of the Club last minute. As part of Mr Abramovich's objective to find a good custodian for Chelsea FC, he has however encouraged each bidder throughout this process to commit investing in the Club – including in the Academy, Women's team, necessary redevelopment of the stadium as well as maintaining the work of Chelsea Foundation.

Following sanctions and other restrictions imposed on Mr

Abramovich by the UK since announcing that the Club would be sold, the loan has also become subject to EU sanctions, requiring additional approvals. That means that the funds will be frozen and subject to a legal procedure governed by authorities. These funds are still earmarked for the Foundation. The Government are aware of these restrictions as well as the legal implications.

To be clear, Mr Abramovich has no access or control of these funds and will not have any access or control of these funds following the sale. Despite the changing circumstances since his initial announcement – he remains committed to finding a good custodian for Chelsea FC and making sure the proceeds go to good causes."

The next day the following statement was released by the club, and news regarding the takeover we'd all been waiting for.

"Chelsea Football Club can confirm that terms have been agreed for a new ownership group, led by Todd Boehly, Clearlake Capital, Mark Walter and Hansjoerg Wyss, to acquire the Club.

Of the total investment being made, £2.5bn will be applied to purchase the shares in the Club and such proceeds will be deposited into a frozen UK bank account with the intention to donate 100% to charitable causes as confirmed by Roman Abramovich. UK Government approval will be required for the proceeds to be transferred from the frozen UK bank account.

In addition, the proposed new owners will commit £1.75bn in further investment for the benefit of the Club. This includes investments in Stamford Bridge, the Academy, the Women's Team and Kingsmeadow and continued funding for the Chelsea Foundation.

The sale is expected to complete in late May subject to all necessary regulatory approvals. More details will be provided at that time."

Todd Boehly would be in attendance for the Wolves game but their manager Bruno Lage would not be as he tested positive for Covid-19. Wolves were in poor form and as the league table stood they had nothing to really play for. We needed a response from the defeat at Everton and secure a top four finish with both Arsenal and Tottenham gaining ground on us.

I took my boy Jack to this game although it was touch and go for a few days leading up to it as he wasn't well. We made it and I felt quietly confident we'd get the win. The last two matches against them had finished 0-0 and after a pretty uneventful first-half you'd be forgiven for thinking the result could be the same. We did however have the ball in the net twice before the break through Werner who was desperately unlucky as he was adjudged to have fouled a defender before he finished well and a Loftus-Cheek close-range goal was cancelled out by VAR.

After the break it was much more lively with the returning Romelu Lukaku scoring two early second-half goals in just two minutes. A penalty after he was fouled in the area with the referee taking to the screen and a great long-range shot into the corner. I don't think anyone could have predicted what would happen next as Chelsea appeared in cruise control. A wonderful individual goal from Trincao with ten minutes to go gave Wolves hope. Defensively we looked more and more uncomfortable and in the final minute of injury time Conor Coady headed in the equaliser. A hugely frustrating result and a game we should have won.

11th May
Premier League
Leeds United 0-3 Chelsea
Elland Road
Attendance: 36,549

Chelsea (3-4-3): Mendy, Chalobah, Christensen, Rudiger, James (Azpilicueta 78), Jorginho (c), Kovacic (Loftus-Cheek 30), Alonso, Mount, Lukaku, Pulisic (Ziyech 78)
Chelsea Goals: Mount (4), Pulisic (55), Lukaku (83)

Leeds United (4-2-3-1): Meslier, Koch, Llorente, Cooper (c), Struijk, Bate (Klich 59), Phillips, Raphinha (Gelhardt (78), James, Harrison, (Firpo 37), Rodrigo

Building up to the game there were reports of a 'bust up' between Tuchel and Alonso during the Wolves match which Thomas said was quickly resolved. The players were initially given a day off in the week but they were soon told to come back in as work was most definitely needed to be done as our league form was now slightly concerning. Despite three league games to go and the F.A Cup Final to come it was announced that Antonio Rudiger would be leaving Chelsea at the end of the season having signed a five year deal at Real Madrid.

Leeds were battling relegation and desperately needed a win and we needed to secure Champions League football with Arsenal just one point behind us now. The atmosphere was going to be loud at Elland Road and they were always going to try and make it as intimidating as possible. However, that crowd was silenced in just the fourth minute with a wonderful goal from Mason Mount. On the half hour mark Mateo Kovacic was substituted off after a horror tackle from Dan James. It earnt the Welshman a red card.

Going into half-time we were in complete control and it didn't take long for our second to come through Christian Pulisic who scored with ease. Romelu Lukaku was looking a real threat and showing some of his early season form. He scored with just a few minutes remaining from close-range to secure the much-needed three points. Mason Mount became the youngest Chelsea player to have double digits in goals and assists in the same Premier League season. It was also Chelsea's first league double over Leeds since the 1988/89 season.

It was a great night for Chelsea with our supporters in full voice. The only downside for us was the injury to Mateo Kovacic with the F.A Cup Final just a few days away. The morning after the match the club announced a new sleeve sponsorship deal for the 2022/23 season with Whale Fin, the digital asset platform powered by the Amber Group. All eyes were now firmly on Liverpool at Wembley.

14th May
F.A Cup Final
Chelsea 0-0 Liverpool (Liverpool won 6-5 on penalties)
Wembley Stadium
Attendance: 84,897

Chelsea (3-4-3): Mendy, Chalobah (Azpilicueta 105), Thiago Silva, Rudiger, James, Jorginho (c), Kovacic (Kante 66), Alonso, Mount, Lukaku (Ziyech 85), Pulisic (Loftus-Cheek 105) (Barkley 119)

Liverpool (4-3-3): Alisson, Alexander-Arnold, Konate, Van Dijk (Matip 91), Robertson (Tsimikas 111), Thiago, Henderson (c), Keita (Milner 74), Salah (Jota 33), Mane, Diaz (Firmino 98)

Another domestic cup final ended in heartbreak on penalties against Liverpool. Thomas Tuchel got his tactics spot on as he did in the Carabao Cup Final, despite the disappointment we went toe-to-toe with a very good Liverpool side that were in the hunt for a quadruple. Marcos Alonso came closest for Chelsea, hitting the cross bar, and at the end of the 90 minutes Liverpool hit both posts.

A stressful game as they usually are but not that much goal mouth action in a very nervy encounter with wasteful finishing on both sides. It had the look of a final that would be decided by penalties. Alonso opened the shootout scoring low to the left and despite Mendy getting a hand to Milner's effort it was 1-1. Azpilicueta hit the post before Thiago scored. James went down the middle before Firminio made it 2-3. Ross Barkley came on in extra-time and took his penalty very well. Alexander-Arnold made it 3-4, Jorginho scored his and Mane was on course to win it for Liverpool. Mendy saved to his left and gave momentum to Chelsea going into sudden death. Ziyech scored and so did Jota. Alission saved low from Mason Mount and Tsimikas scored the winning penalty.

Despite the defeat Thomas Tuchel stated, "Like in the last final, the Carabao Cup, no regrets. I told the team I was proud".

It was very deflating to lose again in the same way but the team left everything on the field. Chelsea had now played 61 games during the season, and a club record six games went to extra-time.

19th May
Premier League
Chelsea 1-1 Leicester City
Stamford Bridge
Attendance: 31,478

Chelsea (3-4-3): Mendy, Chalobah, Thiago Silva, Rudiger, James, Jorginho (c), Kante (Loftus-Cheek 72), Alonso, Ziyech, Lukaku (Havertz 78), Pulisic (Azpilicueta 72)
Chelsea Goal: Alonso (34)

Leicester City (3-5-2): Schmeichel (c), Fofana, Evans, Amartey, Castagne, Maddison, Mendy, Dewsbury-Hall, Thomas, Iheanacho (Barnes 63), Vardy (Perez 78)
Leicester City Goal: Maddison (6)

It was back to Stamford Bridge on the Thursday night for our rearranged fixture against Leicester City. Champions League qualification had already been confirmed thanks to Newcastle beating Arsenal in the Monday night football. However, despite our game in hand Tottenham were just one point behind us so guaranteeing third place was our motivation.

News regarding Todd Boehly's Chelsea takeover was once again conflicting, with stumbling blocks reported, before the rumours were later denied, with official confirmation imminent.

The drinks were certainly flowing pre-match in the Cock Tavern pub with a really good atmosphere, reflecting on the season it felt in some ways the match would interrupt a great social.

The game and atmosphere had a real end of season feel to it and that was apparent with the attendance and Leicester failing to sell out their full allocation. The Shed End unveiled a large crowd-surfer of Thomas Tuchel saying 'Deutscher Maestro' which he most certainly approved. The game matched the occasion with a very lethargic performance. We dominated possession but found ourselves 1-0 down after just six minutes with a well-taken goal from James Maddison. Marcos Alonso equalised ten minutes before half-time on the volley after a wonderful pass from the ever-consistent Reece James.

In the second-half we kept pushing for the winner but again it was wasteful finishing after dominating possession. Christian Pulisic in particular had a glorious chance to win it for us. The points were shared and due to our inferior goal difference third place was secured with just one more game remaining.

The next day Antonio Rudiger released an open letter to supporters about him leaving at the end of the season. "Chelsea will always be in my heart... Yes, I've heard abuse, but I also felt the love. At the end of the day, the light was stronger than the darkness. For that, I will always be Chelsea."

22nd May
Premier League
Chelsea 2-1 Watford
Stamford Bridge
Attendance: 32,089

Chelsea (3-4-3): Mendy, Azpilicueta (c), Thiago Silva, Rudiger (Barkley 65), James, Kante, Saul, Kenedy (Sarr 59), Ziyech, Havertz, Mount (Chilwell 90)
Chelsea Goals: Havertz (11), Barkley (90)

Watford (4-5-1): Bachmann, Femenia, Kabasele, Samir, Kamara (Masina 77), King (Hernandez 72), Sissoko (c), Kayembe (Gosling 82), Cleverley, Sema, Joao Pedro
Watford Goal: Gosling (87)

The final game of the season saw Chelsea take on already relegated Watford at Stamford Bridge. With my dad away it was a chance to go with my son Jack for the final time this season. Referee Mike Dean would officiate his final game before retiring. The team selection raised a few eyebrows with fringe players being given opportunities rather than players from the academy.

The atmosphere in the ground was pretty decent considering Watford were already relegated and third place was already secured for The Blues. 'We Are The Shed' unveiled a wonderful Chelsea montage of past players, coaches and owners, absolutely amazing! Kai Havertz got us off to the perfect start with a tap-in after some good work from Kenedy.

As expected Chelsea were dominant throughout but wasteful with chances. On 65 minutes Antonio Rudiger was substituted off, in what would be his last game for the club, with the whole of Stamford Bridge on their feet. Throughout the second-half most people in the stadium were talking about what was happening in the title race and wanting to know the score updates. As it happens Chelsea fans at one stage were singing 'Come on City' as we desperately didn't want Liverpool to win it.

Whilst all that was going on Watford equalised through Dan Gosling but no one seemed remotely bothered. However, my son Jack was and after his last two games against Brentford and Wolves I was desperate for him to see a win. Ben Chilwell came on towards the end to another standing ovation after missing most of the season. Boy, have we missed him!

Just as it looked like it would be yet another home draw Ross Barkley headed in a Reece James cross in injury time. Jack lifted high into the air with us both being delighted. We finished the season with a win and the team did their usual lap of honour on the final game.

Manchester City won the league on the final day coming back dramtically to beat Aston Villa 3-2 after trailing 2-0. Liverpool missed out by a point and Chelsea finished third, three points clear of Tottenham who finished fourth ahead of North London rivals Arsenal. Manchester United occupied the Europa Conference League place and Burnley joined Watford and Norwich in relegation after a remarkable escape from Leeds.

The following days saw the Premier League and UK Government approve the sale of Chelsea Football Club to the Todd Boehly led Clearlake consortium. The club and Roman Abramovich finally confirmed the sale.

28th May

"It has been nearly three months since I announced my intention to sell Chelsea FC. During this time, the team have worked hard to find the right custodian for Chelsea FC that would be best positioned to successfully lead the Club into its next chapter.

The ownership of this Club comes with great responsibility. Since I came to Chelsea nearly 20 years ago, I have witnessed first-hand what this Club can achieve. My goal has been to ensure that the next owner has a mindset that will enable success for the Men's and Women's team, as well as the will and drive to continue developing other key aspects of the Club, such as the Academy and the vital work of Chelsea Foundation.

I am pleased this search has now come to a successful conclusion. As I hand over Chelsea to its new custodians, I would like to wish them the best of success, both on and off the pitch. It has been an honour of a lifetime to be a part of this Club - I would like to thank all the Club's past and current players, staff, and of course fans for these incredible years. I am proud that as a result of our joint successes, millions of people will now benefit from the new charitable foundation which is being established. This is the legacy which we have created together.

Thank you.

Roman"

30th May

The consortium led by Todd Boehly, chairman and CEO of Eldridge, and Clearlake Capital Group, L.P. (together with its affiliates, "Clearlake"), today announced completion of the ownership transfer of Chelsea Football Club ("Chelsea FC" or "the Club"). The consortium also includes Hansjörg Wyss, founder of the Wyss Foundation, and Mark Walter, co-founder and CEO of Guggenheim Capital. Walter and Boehly are owners of the Los Angeles Dodgers, the Los Angeles Lakers, and the Los Angeles Sparks. The transaction has received all necessary approvals from The Government of the United Kingdom, The Premier

League, and other authorities.

Under the terms of the agreement, Boehly and Clearlake will share joint control and equal governance of the Club. Boehly will serve as Chairman of the holding company. Boehly and Clearlake are committed to investing in key areas that will extend and enhance Chelsea's competitiveness, including the redevelopment of Stamford Bridge, further investment in the Academy, the Women's Team and Kingsmeadow stadium. The owners will also continue the important work of the Chelsea Foundation.

"We are honoured to become the new custodians of Chelsea Football Club," said Boehly. "We're all in 100% every minute of every match. Our vision as owners is clear, we want to make the fans proud. Along with our commitment to developing the youth squad and acquiring the best talent, our plan of action is to invest in the Club for the long-term and build on Chelsea's remarkable history of success. I personally want to thank ministers and officials in the British government, and the Premier League, for all their work in making this happen."

Behdad Eghbali and José E. Feliciano, Clearlake co-founders and managing partners, said, "We are excited to commit the resources to continue Chelsea's leading role in English and global football, and as an engine for football talent development. We also want to thank the authorities for all their work throughout the process. As pioneers in sports and media investing, we are thrilled to partner with Todd and the rest of the consortium to meaningfully grow the Club as a global platform. Together, we will expand the Club's investment across infrastructure, technology, and sports science to support the incredible Chelsea football and commercial teams - all with the goal of leveraging this growth to fuel even more on-pitch success. The new ownership group wishes to recognise the dedication and professionalism of the Department for Digital, Culture, Media and Sport, HM Treasury, and the Premier League in conducting their reviews of this historic and complex transaction."

Deutsche Bank, Goldman Sachs, Moelis & Company LLC, and Robey Warshaw LP served as financial advisors to the new ownership group. Latham & Watkins LLP, Paul, Weiss, Rifkind,

Wharton & Garrison LP, and Sidley Austin LLP served as legal counsel. The Raine Group served as exclusive financial advisor to Fordstam Limited and Chelsea FC. Northridge Law LLP, Simmons & Simmons LP, and Pillsbury, Winthrop, Shaw, Pittman LP served as legal counsel.

SUMMARY

Only Chelsea could be crowned Champions Of The World and be sanctioned by the UK Governement in the same season. Chelsea played 63 games out of a possible 66 at the start of the season. A third place finish and Champions League qualification secured as we limped over the line. Romelu Lukaku wasn't the prolific goal scorer we hoped him to be and his interview with the Italian press didn't help. Chelsea were one of two Premier League teams who didn't have a game postponed due to Covid-19 cases, as well as key injuries this added more pressure to Tuchel who handled himself impeccably throughout the season. The Super Cup and Club World Cup were secured early on, and Chelsea only missed out on two domestic cups losing to Liverpool on penalties. Mason Mount was announced as Player Of The Year and I'm sure Thiago Silva would've been a very close second. The sale of the club finally happened at the end of the season, there really is never a dull moment at Stamford Bridge.

GATE 17
THE COMPLETE COLLECTION
(SUMMER 2022)

CHELSEA
Over Land and Sea – Mark Worrall
Chelsea here, Chelsea There – Kelvin Barker, David Johnstone, Mark Worrall
Chelsea Football Fanzine – the best of 'cfcuk'
One Man Went to Mow – Mark Worrall
Making History Not Reliving It –
Kelvin Barker, David Johnstone, Mark Worrall
Celery! Representing Chelsea in the 1980s – Kelvin Barker
Stuck On You, a year in the life of a Chelsea supporter – Walter Otton
Palpable Discord, a year of drama and dissent at Chelsea – Clayton Beerman
Rhyme and Treason – Carol Ann Wood
Eddie Mac Eddie Mac – Eddie McCreadie's Blue & White Army
The Italian Job, A Chelsea thriller starring Antonio Conte – Mark Worrall
Carefree! Chelsea Chants & Terrace Culture – Mark Worrall, Walter Otton
Diamonds, Dynamos and Devils – Tim Rolls
Arrivederci Antonio, The Italian Job (part two) – Mark Worrall
Where Were You When We Were Shocking? – Neil L. Smith
Chelsea, 100 Memorable Matches – Chelsea Chadder
Bewitched, Bothered & Bewildered – Carol Ann Wood
Stamford Bridge Is Falling Down – Tim Rolls
Cult Fiction – Dean Mears
Chelsea, If Twitter Was Around When… – Chelsea Chadder
Blue Army – Vince Cooper
Liquidator 1969-70 A Chelsea Memoir – Mark Worrall
When Skies Are Grey, Super Frank, Chelsea And The Coronavirus Crisis – Mark Worrall
Tales Of The (Chelsea) Unexpected – David Johnstone & Neil L Smith
The Ultimate Unofficial Chelsea Quiz Book – Chelsea Chadder
Blue Days – Chris Wright
Let The Celery Decide – Walter Otton
Blue Hitmen – Paul Radcliffe
Sexton For God – Tim Rolls
Tales From The Shed – Edited by Mark Worrall
For Better Or Worse – Jason Gibbins
Come Along And Sing This Song – Johnny Neal's Blue And White Army
Days (I'll Remember All My Life) – Kelvin Barker
End Of An Era: Chelsea 2021-2022 – Chris Wright

FICTION
Blue Murder, Chelsea Till I Die – Mark Worrall
The Wrong Outfit – Al Gregg
The Red Hand Gang – Walter Otton
Coming Clean – Christopher Morgan
This Damnation – Mark Worrall
Poppy – Walter Otton

NON FICTION
Roe2Ro – Walter Otton
Shorts – Walter Otton
England International Football Team Quiz & Trivia Book – George Cross

www.gate17books.co.uk

Made in United States
Orlando, FL
14 September 2022

22412844R10086